REENGINEERING THE BANK

A Blueprint for Survival and Success

REVISED EDITION

REENGINEERING THE BANK

A Blueprint for Survival and Success

Paul H. Allen

McGraw-Hill

New York   San Francisco   Washington, DC   Aukland   Bogotá
Caracas   Lisbon   London   Madrid   Mexico City   Milan
Montreal   New Delhi   San Juan   Singapore
Sydney   Tokyo   Toronto

Library of Congress Cataloging-in-Publication Data

Allen, Paul H. (Paul Howard), 1954–
   Reengineering the bank : a blueprint for suirval and success /
Paul H. Allen, Lisa Kofed. — Rev. ed.
      p.   cm.
   Includes index.
   ISBN 0-7863-1111-8 (alk. paper)
   1. Bank management.   2. Banks and banking—United States.
3. Organizational change.   4. Reengineering (Management)—United
States.   I. Kofed, Lisa.   II. Title.
HG1615.A537   1997
332.1´068´4—dc21   97–1289

McGraw-Hill

A Division of The *McGraw-Hill* Companies

1 2 3 4 5 6 7 8 9 0 DOC/DOC 9 0 9 8 7

ISBN 0-7863-1111-8

Printed and bound by R.R. Donnelley & Sons Company.

This publication is designed to provide accurate and
authoritative information in regard to the subject matter
covered. It is sold with the understanding that neither the
author nor the publisher is engaged in rendering legal, accounting,
or other professional service. If legal advice or other expert
assistance is required, the services of a competent professional
person should be sought.
—*From a Declaration of Principles jointly adopted by a committee
of the American Bar Association and a Committee of Publishers.*

McGraw-Hill books are available at special quantity discounts to use as
premiums and sales promotions, or for use in corporate training programs.
for more information, please write to the Director of Special Sales, McGraw-Hill, 11
West 19th Street, New York, NY 10011. Or contact your
local bookstore.

For Sandra, Elva, Mark, and Emma and, of course, my father, Bill, whose indomitable spirit following the War has been my ultimate inspiration.

CONTENTS

Chapter 4

HOW TO REENGINEER

Chapter 5

Chapter 6

Chapter 7

Chapter 8

ACKNOWLEDGMENTS

The years 1992 to 1996 have been banner years for bank profitability. Aided by the Federal Reserve's outstanding management of interest rates, U.S. banks have come back from the brink of disaster. And, other than in Japan, the global industry's returns have rebounded. Proposing radical reengineering of banks today may therefore seem mistimed.

More and more superior performers, however, are acknowledging that their vision of the future requires immediate action. They are leading their institutions to a new economic plateau, one that will help ensure they remain profitable and competitive into the twenty-first century.

My approach to working in tandem with bank management to reengineer their institutions has been the result of 15 years of evolving thought and experimentation—thanks to the outstanding executives who have provided pragmatic challenges to my conceptual ideas.

For this, I am particularly indebted to: Terry Larsen and Chuck Coltman of CoreStates Financial Corporation, Philadelphia; Spence Eccles and Morgan Evans of First Security Corporation, Salt Lake City; Oliver Waddell and Joe Campanella of Star Banc Corporation, Cincinnati; Mac McDonald and Gaylon Layfield of Signet Financial Corporation; William Balderston III of Lincoln First, Rochester; and Ian Paterson, formerly of the Forward Trust Group and Standard Chartered Bank; among other banking industry leaders.

Special thanks is owed to those of my colleagues at Aston, who have burnt the midnight oil in supporting my writing of this book, notably Jacqueline Corbelli, Mark Elletson, Jeff Friedel, Jay Kalawar, Oliver Sommer, Larry Krasner, Alex Barros, and Victoria Chu. Their good humor in undertaking this challenge in addition to already demanding workloads went above and beyond the call of duty. This is especially true of Lisa Kofod, whose patience in deciphering countless pages scribbled or dictated while on airplanes, and in accepting draft after draft for amendment, was exceptional.

Finally, I owe a debt of gratitude to my publisher, McGraw Hill; to my friend, Philip Recchia, for his outstanding editorial services; and, of course, to Sandra, Mark and Emma, who lived through the crazy hours of the book's composition.

Paul Allen is chairman of Aston Associates, the Greenwich, Connecticut-based bank investment and redesign firm founded in 1990. He has successfully reengineered over 12 major banking institutions worldwide. Mr. Allen was formerly one of the leading partners in the financial institutions practice of McKinsey & Co, working in both the New York and the European offices. He earned an MBA from the Harvard Business School, where he was a Harkness Fellow and a Baker Scholar, and a MA in Law from Oxford University. Three recent redesign efforts show the impact of Aston Associates' reengineering expertise:

- **CoreStates Financial Corp (Philadelphia):** Since November 1994, Paul Allen's redesign of CoreStates has added $3.8 billion in market capitalization (110 percent increase in stock price) for this $46 billion bank. CoreStates has achieved cost savings of $180 million and revenue gains of $40 million. CoreStates' efficiency ratio fell from 60 percent to 53 percent from September 1994 to December 1996.

- **First Security Bancorp (Utah):** Since the involvement of Aston with this $14 billion bank holding company in May 1995, the stock price has risen 120 percent from $15 to $34, adding $1.5 billion to market capital. Redesign results totaled $40 million in process cost impact and $25 million in increased revenues. In the first year of implementation, First Security's efficiency ratio declined from 64 percent to 58 percent. Salomon Brothers selected First Security as one of four banks in the U.S. among its "The Best the World Has to Offer: Global Picks for 1997."

- **Star Banc Corporation (Ohio):** Aston's involvement in the reengineering of Star helped lead to a 240 percent increase in share value between August 1992 and December 1996, adding over $1.9 billion in shareholder value. As of March 1997 Star had improved its return on assets to 1.8 percent, its return on equity to 21.7 percent, and its efficiency ratio from 63 to 48 percent. *The Wall Street Journal* recently elected StarBanc to its "Shareholder Scoreboard Honor Roll" for its sustained stock performance over the last five years.

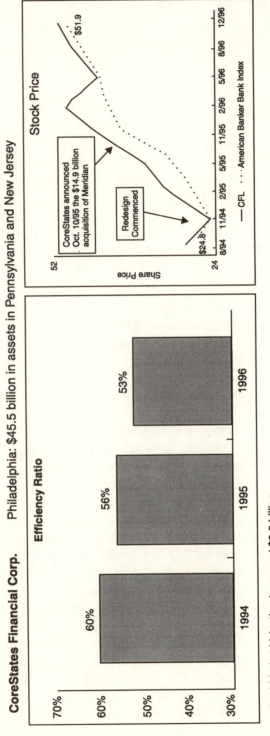

CoreStates Financial Corp.   Philadelphia: $45.5 billion in assets in Pennsylvania and New Jersey

Efficiency Ratio

70%
60%
50%
40%
30%

60% 1994
56% 1995
53% 1996

Total Market Valuation increased $3.8 billion.

Stock Price

52
$51.9

CoreStates announced
Oct. 10/95 the $14.9 billion
acquisition of Meridian

Redesign
Commenced

$24.8
24

Share Price

8/94 11/94 2/95 5/95 11/95 2/96 5/96 8/96 12/96

—— CFL   · · · · American Banker Bank Index

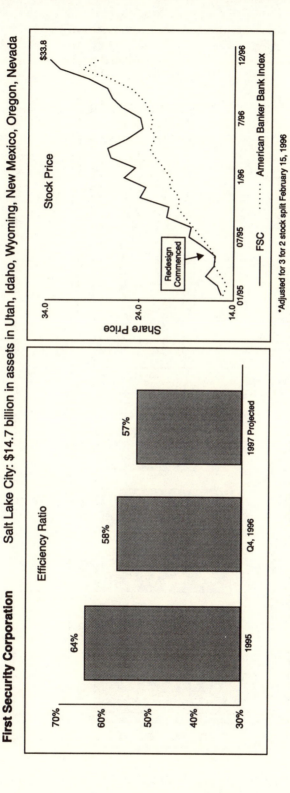

First Security Corporation Salt Lake City: $14.7 billion in assets in Utah, Idaho, Wyoming, New Mexico, Oregon, Nevada

Efficiency Ratio

64% — 1995
58% — Q4, 1996
57% — 1997 Projected

Stock Price

——— FSC ⋯⋯ American Banker Bank Index

*Adjusted for 3 for 2 stock split February 15, 1996

Total Market Valuation increased $1.5 billion. For the period 4/95–12/96 American Banker Bank Index rose 84% while First Security rose 118%.

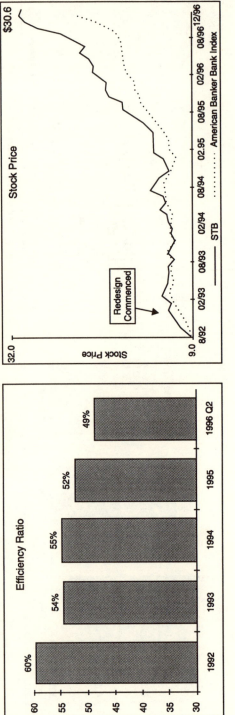

Star Banc Corporation Cincinnati: $10.1 billion in assets in Ohio, Indiana, Kentucky

Efficiency Ratio

Stock Price

Total Market Valuation increased $1.9 billion 37% CGR. For the period 8/92–12/96 American Bank Index rose 145% while Star Banc rose 253%.

INTRODUCTION

Salomon Brothers interviewed more than 50 leading banks in 11 major banking markets to "evaluate the industry's success in controlling costs and to determine how performance might improve in the future."[1] They concluded that:

> Cost management has become a dominant strategic theme throughout the banking world. Buffeted by asset quality problems, weak loan demand and the difficulty of building reliable non-interest income streams, bank managements have almost universally turned to cost reduction as one of the principal drivers of earnings growth. . . . The major lesson from the handful of successful low cost producers is that a cultural commitment to cost management, invariably driven forcefully throughout the organization by the chief executive, is the single most important success factor. . . . Cost reduction runs counter to the culture of most banking organizations, and the will to maximize profits through what effectively constitutes staff reduction and repositioning is necessary to achieve durable results. If this culture is in place, the techniques of successful cost management are proven and straightforward. . . . Most such efforts are summarized under the heading "business process reengineering." . . . The use of these techniques is spreading rapidly as banks in one market after another acknowledge that . . . cost reduction [is] one of the few realistic means of achieving profit growth.

I would add that repricing of services based on the "perceived" value banks provide to customers is comparably important to successful future competition.

An imperative to redesign fundamentally the way in which bankers operate is a worldwide phenomenon. Previously discrete financial service industries are converging and competing aggressively on each other's turf. Regulatory barriers, which had impeded both inter-bank competition and non-bank entry into the most lucrative of banking markets, have crumbled. Ever-accelerating product and technological innovation require rapid

---

1   *Cost Management in Global Banking—The Lessons of Low Cost Producers,* Salomon Brothers, October 1993.

responses and huge bets on the future. The leeway to price in an unsophisticated "bundled" fashion has disappeared as customers shop for each of their individual product needs.

All of these trends (and more) are creating an environment for the banking industry where the margin of error for underperformance is continually narrowing—as evidenced by the global impact of misconceived real-estate lending and the rapid penetration by product-specific suppliers, such as mutual funds, credit cards like the Discover card, captive auto finance companies, and commercial paper underwriters.

Yet bank costs are almost always too high and their prices too low. In the past, regulation prevented the development of a discipline that would inspire bankers constantly to challenge arcane, redundant, or duplicative processes—this at an enormous cost. Pricing has, at best, been on a cost-plus or competitor-matching basis. The earnings left on the table are in the order of $45 billion, pretax, annually in the United States alone.

And this is as true for a universal bank in Frankfurt, or a city bank in Tokyo, as it is for a regional bank in Boston. The specific process misdesigns may differ, but the detritus of the past is present across the board. It is time to remove these historical burdens. In institutions both large and small, I have seen the reinvigoration of staff and corporate culture take place once the gloves are removed and employees are empowered to look at existing processes with a "clean sheet of paper" mentality.

GLOBAL EFFICIENCY FOCUS AT A GLANCE

Since this book was first published, the imperative to realign costs and revenues in banks has become recognized around the world. The following thumbnail case studies illustrate the emerging focus on efficiency ratio (roughly, cents of operating cost to generate each dollar of revenue) at many of the leading banks worldwide.

Australia

The perception of management of the top-performing Australian banks appears to be that work measurement-type techniques have been exhausted, and further efficiencies will rely on process redesign. A constraint may be resistance to further layoffs because of a tenure mentality among unionized employees.

- With an ultimate efficiency goal of 45 percent, **National Australia Bank** has internalized cost consciousness. For example, its "value-based management" has led to the use of a reporting system that facilitates the daily allocation of personnel by branch based on performance measures. Other factors in the bank's superior ranking include its information technology, its customer focus, and its consolidation of retail product offerings. Further efficiencies will arise from modernizing branch processing from a partially automated variant of early twentieth century practices, including the consolidation of transaction-processing centers.

- **Australia and New Zealand Banking Group** initially focused on an activity-based management review of support personnel as part of an overall operational restructuring. They then focused on operational improvements and the reduction of technical staff. Thirteen area level operations centers will be consolidated into six state-level centers and branch networks will be rationalized and electronic delivery channels further refined.

- To control expenses, **Westpac** has instituted continuous management reviews against work performance standards and is redesigning branch processing.

Austria

- **Creditanstalt-Bankverein** uses financial incentives to generate suggestions from employees for process improvements. Top management salaries have been reduced, specific headcount reductions targeted, data centers consolidated, loan applications and other processes reviewed, and information technology investments reconsidered in order to attain better value (e.g., developing unit costing).

- To control headcount, **Z Laenderbank Bank Austria** has developed new, performance-based employee compensation programs, introduced flexi-time and developed a "best practices" communications program. Budgets and previously-approved programs are constantly reevaluated.

Canada

- **Toronto Dominion Bank** has sought efficiencies through its flat organizational structure, due to its relatively higher concentration of branches in Ontario and to its complete systems overhaul in the late 1980s. It avoided paying a high premium for a securities firm, unlike most of its competitors, by taking a *de novo* approach. By emphasizing the early introduction of new technology-based products, it has been able to amass market share quickly.

• **Royal Bank of Canada** (RBC) takes the approach of optimizing the use of expenses to generate revenues. For example, using cheaper automated teller machine (ATM) envelopes saved $1 million. With its major technology improvements largely completed, it is seeking process improvements in transactions processing and servicing alternative delivery channels. It has been successful in consolidating branches and operations centers and is undertaking headquarters process improvements in credit, retail branch administration, finance, and other administrative functions. With Toronto Dominion and Bank of Montreal, RBC has recently announced the creation of a stand-alone enterprise to "co-source" high-volume transaction processing.

• **Bank of Nova Scotia** has relatively less divisionalization and significantly smaller central and regional staff groups than its competitors, as well as a firmly ingrained cost culture. Its expenses and capital expenditures are approved centrally, and projected cost savings are audited. The bank's attitude toward technology is to delay minor improvements and invest heavily in major improvements. For example, its $100 million operations restructuring will use clusters, significantly eliminate paper-based branch processing, combine deposit and loan officer positions, and further automate platform customer service and sales.

• **Bank of Montreal's** "Continuous Improvement" process includes annual goal setting and tracking of expense-related items by business unit. It has combined operations centers, reduced management layers, and begun restructuring its U.S. subsidiary, Harris BankCorp.

• After completing a major systems overhaul and taking a large restructuring charge, **Canadian Imperial Bank of Commerce** has embarked on a basic redesign of its retail network and corporate staff with the intent of reducing bureaucracy. It has merged its corporate and investment banking units, transferred small commercial accounts to retail, and rationalized its international business, moving toward centralized operations. The bank has also begun consolidating previously decentralized retail operations and is closing mature, rural branch locations that are subscale.

France

French labor union activism hampers restructuring, requiring banks to rely on reduced recruiting and attrition.

- **Credit Industriel et Commercial** implemented a large staff reduction and renovation program in the early 1990s.
- **Credit Commercial de France** has successfully negotiated with its unions to manage staffing levels. An internal system of expense negotiations among cost and profit centers, where cost centers that do not offer competitive prices may be scaled back or eliminated, has been created to achieve efficiency improvements.
- **Credit Lyonnais** employs more traditional time-and-motion studies to control expenses. Economies may be achieved as high-technology spending realizes projected savings.
- **Banque Indosuez** is seeking to extend the impact of a one-time cost-reduction program. It is restructuring its back-office and wire transfer operations, centralizing other operations, outsourcing, and decentralizing responsibility for certain systems.

Germany

Organizational restructuring has taken place among German banks as geographic loyalties have diminished in importance and the imposition of cost controls at the manager level have become a priority.

- **Deutsche Bank** has restructured its branch and headquarters staffs to distribute better cost management responsibilities among managers and it has focused on restructuring its cash-transfer processes. Other efficiency measures include: data-center consolidation; replacing tellers with ATMs; and requiring support staff to justify their services, especially data processing.

In total, by year-end 1996, Deutsche expects to reduce domestic staff by 20 percent from 1992 levels.

◆ **Commerzbank** is emphasizing targeting market niches and cross-selling products while reducing personnel.

◆ **Dresdner Bank** is beginning to segment its branch network, migrate its retail securities customers to mutual funds, and centralize operations.

Hong Kong

◆ The low efficiency ratio of the **HongkongBank** unit of **Hongkong and Shanghai Banking Corp** reflects low headquarters staffing, imposed obstacles to the addition of non-revenue-generating staff, and significant automation. There is widespread use of electronic retail delivery in its markets, and operations have been centralized with its affiliate, **Hang Seng Bank**.

Japan

Cost control is emphasized more by Japanese wholesale and investment banks than by the retail banks. The latter made significant technology investments in the early 1980s, resulting in a high level of centralized, automated retail transaction processing. Other factors affecting efficiency in Japan include high service fees paid by consumers, offset by the burden of the many unconsolidated subsidiaries of the banks. The burden of nonperforming real-estate credits and trading losses, with the resulting bank and credit union failures, will focus ever-increasing attention of Japanese bankers on process redesign, with an inevitable challenge to "lifelong employment."[2]

◆ **Sumitomo Bank** is reducing its retail staffing levels, while expanding deposit product offerings directed at high net-worth individuals. It is moving much of its processing into subsidiaries that can pay lower than union wage. The bank is also consolidating treasury, project finance, and other functions overseas.

---

2   See also Ian Orton, *Reengineered Banks,* Lafferty Publications, 1995.

- **Sanwa Bank**, one of the lowest-cost producers among Japan's five major city banks, has benefited from the extensive deployment of ATMs in unmanned branches.
- **Fuji Bank** will slow new branch openings, consolidate branches and increase its percentage of automated branches. It intends to reduce overtime and decrease the rate of increase in its headcount.
- **Industrial Bank of Japan** will halve its information technology and communications expense and pare new branch openings.
- **Bank of Tokyo** has assiduously controlled expenses by increasing the use of temporary staff; simplifying products; restructuring processes; and centralizing accounting, operations, information, and services. It is not clear what consolidation impact will be achieved through the merger with Mitsubishi Bank Ltd.

Netherlands

- **ABN/Amro** is evaluating new distribution channels as a key method to develop operating economies. For example, special agents in a new subsidiary originate residential mortgages. In addition, ATMs will soon conduct half of all domestic electronic transfers, partially as a result of financial incentives offered to customers to migrate them toward automation. The bank is also outsourcing certain functions and centralizing data centers.

Spain and Portugal

There is wide historical performance disparity and a lack of discernible trends in Spanish and Portuguese banks' management of efficiency ratios.

- **Banco Popular Español** has restrained headcount growth for over 15 years, despite its rapid growth. The bank has a lean headquarters staff, and it generally pays employees less than competitors, while maintaining a low turnover rate. New systems will eliminate the need for batch branch processing.
- **Banco Santander**, which was late in determining the necessity for process improvements, is restructuring its branch system by opening limited product branches to improve item processing and reduce headcount.

◆ **Banco Bilbao Vizcaya** has reduced staff by the maximum
allowable under union agreements since it was formed in a 1988
merger. It monitors merger-related cost savings through a
rigorous budgeting process. Other productivity improvements
include regionalized retail operations centers which may be
supplanted as new systems permit realtime branch processing.

◆ **Banco Comercial Português**, a 1980s start-up bank, has
different delivery systems for each of six different client
segments. Its management information system provides daily
product, customer, and profit-center profitability reporting.

Switzerland

The large Swiss banks have been restructuring and shrinking their retail
networks, using headcount controls and analytical productivity measures,
automating processes, reducing staff, standardizing product lines, and
migrating customers to automated services.

◆ **Swiss Bank Corporation** (SBC) has relied on centralizing
smaller units' operations in existing regional centers and
consolidating documentary credits in fewer centers. It has also
standardized products and effectively used automated
productivity measures in managing its network. Also, price
incentives have encouraged customers to prepare their own
documentation. SBC recently announced reductions of 1,700
positions, closure of a quarter of its branches, and consolidation
from fifteen to three regional centers.

◆ **Credit Suisse** (CS) has effectively used automation to restructure
business and branch processes. It has a smaller branch network
than competitors with regionalized operations centers. This year
CS Holding has targeted 3,500 Swiss job reductions as part of a
5,000 rationalization worldwide.

◆ **Union Bank of Switzerland** is slightly behind competitors in
consolidating its retail operations, but is centralizing into eight
centers, along with some product-specific facilities. It is
somewhat hampered in reducing its information technology staff
as a result of its tendency toward systems customization.

United Kingdom

UK banks have led Europe in cost reduction, having closed branches and reduced staff through attrition and early retirement programs. However, paper processes still dominate in UK branch systems, and in-market mergers have been concentrated among the building societies.

- **Midland Bank** has made considerable staff reductions and has closed many branches. It is attempting to use its bank-by-phone technology, First Direct, as both a cheaper delivery mechanism and a value-added service to a broader customer base.

- **Lloyds Bank** appears most efficient, because of its insurance and other fee income, and is continuing to reduce headcount, particularly in its branch network. However, the "reengineering" effort begun in September 1992, for which implementation began in July 1993, appears to have had limited impact. Despite multiple implementation waves, the bank's efficiency ratio has only declined from 64 percent in 1990 to 60 percent in 1995 (even given the TSB merger).

- **National Westminster Bank** began a formal cost-reduction program as early as 1990. It continues to close branches aggressively. Internally, many staff members have been reallocated to insurance, sales, and customer service.

- **Royal Bank of Scotland Group's** Project Columbus has led to projected increases of £200 million of net income improvements by 1997 (40 percent revenues, 45 percent cost reduction, and 15 percent credit loss improvements) with a net staff reduction of 3,500. Project Columbus, combined with the pioneering effort of Direct Line for personal lines insurance sales, has given an excellent basis for redesign.

The global focus on managing bank costs is striking. However, it is unclear whether bankers globally are fundamentally committed to basic redesign of their banks. There is a risk of "moving deck chairs on the Titanic." The systematic review of every process through true reengineering is a daunting challenge, but is also critical to success in the global banking environment.

WHAT IS REENGINEERING?

Reengineering is the redesign of processes from scratch. It is acknowledging that the way in which things have been done in the past is not sacrosanct, and that a new competitive environment and developing technologies require radically new ways of doing things, not merely doing the same old things of the past at lower cost or in better ways—the focus of much of the bank efforts above.

Reengineering is not arbitrary, across-the-board cost cutting, which is often disguised behind euphemisms such as "restructuring," "total quality control," "downsizing," and "horizontal management." Indeed, often the term "reengineering" has itself been used to justify arbitrary cost cutting, to the point where I would almost change the title of this book! Arbitrary programs do not work. Because the volume and nature of tasks has not been reduced or changed, costs creep back through the hiring of temporary employees or through overtime. Staff members become disgruntled, as they know that reasonably efficient departments are penalized for the sake of those that have been mismanaged in the past. Customer service suffers because the easiest areas to reduce are often the "variable" costs of front-line employees.

Nor does reengineering always result in staff reductions in all areas. Costs in banks are dominated by personnel expenses. Fundamental economic redesign does, therefore, often result in substantially lower employee numbers. Such reduction is selective, however, reflecting the relative value added of the processes served by each position. Moreover, the level of natural attrition in banks, if properly harnessed as part of a comprehensive human resources strategy, enables the cost side of the reengineering process to be managed humanely and equitably. No radical redesign can be entirely painless, but anesthetics are available. And they work.

Reengineering the bank, as outlined in this book, is an intense organizational experience, pitting the whole staff against demanding and inviolable deadlines. Nonetheless, it is manageable without compromising service or the bank's strategic objectives. Because the reengineering approach is perceived as fair, and results in the creation of a truly new bank (as opposed to the latest knee-jerk response to meet unexpected earnings), employees become enthusiastic and involved. They put in the extra effort to cover their normal duties, as well as the demands of the program. They want to be part of making "their" bank a winner.

If this sounds Pollyannish, it has nonetheless been true in the 12 reengineering programs that I have assisted. Employees do not like being in the position of feeling embarrassed to go home and talk about how they spent their day. The goals of reengineering are: to create an institution with superior customer service; to place the highest focus on profitable sales opportunities; and to create a culture of "can do," not "can't do, because." If properly structured, and led by committed senior management, these objectives are achievable and will fundamentally enhance bank economics through sustainable annuity earnings (not ephemeral, one-time, arbitrary returns).

I have divided this book into three sections: the first (Chapters 1–4) summarizes why the reengineering imperative has arisen, and when redesign opportunities exist; the second (Chapters 5–9), outlines the specifics of how to carry out a comprehensive reengineering program. The third section provides three case studies of redesign.

The first section is deliberately structured around the experience of U.S. bankers. Nonetheless, I believe readers worldwide will find that most of the observations resonate with regard to their particular markets.

The challenge is great and immediate. The rewards are survival and success in the newly rough-and-tumble world of banking.

U.S. BANK REENGINEERING AT A GLANCE

The enormous opportunities that reengineering affords the U.S. banking industry are evident in the following statistics.[3]

Number of banks in the U.S. as of December 1996	9,500
Total number of major U.S. banks reengineered between 1980 and 1996	220
Average number of major banks that reengineered annually in the United States	13
Average annual increased return on equity per bank as a result of reengineering program	+6%

Potential for Increased U.S. Bank Annual Earnings (Percentage 1996 Pretax Earnings) as a Result of Industrywide Reengineering Programs

Cost	$50 billion (40 percent)
Pricing	$25 billion (20 percent)

---

3   "Bank Reengineering Impact Study," Aston Associates, 1993–1996.

Impact on U.S. Banks Reengineered	Pre-Reengineering	Post-Reengineering
Average ROA	1.0%	1.5%
Average ROE	14%	20%
Average efficiency ratio (Costs/revenues)	63%	50-55%

Top Three Reasons Cited by U.S. Bankers for Undertaking Reengineering Programs 1990–1996

1. Stock price is weak with resulting inability to fend off hostile takeovers, fund acquisitions, or afford technology investments.
2. Efficiency ratio is sub-par (in the 60 to 65 percent range, not 50 to 55 percent).
3. Excessive redundancy of processes becomes apparent.

Top Five Results of U.S. Bank Reengineering Programs since 1990

1. Significantly improved customer service.
2. Reinvigorated corporate culture focused on sales.
3. Delayered management structure with senior managers and decision making "closer to customers."
4. New economic profile with efficiency ratio in the 50–55 percent range.
5. Significantly improved stock price up 20–30 percent within 6 months of completion of the reengineering project, and sustained market outperformance versus peers.

Average duration of reengineering design phase of program	4–9 months
Average length of reengineering program implementation	12–18 months

REENGINEERING THE BANK

A Blueprint for Survival and Success

Why and When to Reengineer

The banking industry faces an imperative to reengineer its cost base and its pricing approach. The historical evolution of the industry has not followed the Darwinian model: natural selection creating an ideal species perfectly suited to exploit its strategic, competitive, and organizational environment. Rather, emerging from the regulatory cocoon of the past, the industry has found itself maladapted to the real world. Costs are too high (spent often on the least-value-added processes, tasks, and services) and misunderstood through arcane, misleading measurement systems. Product and service pricing have been systematically mismanaged, bear little relationship to the determinants of perceived customer value, and face serious regulatory barriers to change.

Section One will briefly outline: first, the history of the industry that has led to this state of affairs, and the resulting implications for the cost and pricing structure of banks (the "why" of the reengineering imperative); and second, the telltale signs of reengineering opportunities (the "when" for reengineering).

CHAPTER 1

Historical Overview

INTRODUCTION

To anyone even peripherally aware of contemporary developments in the banking industry, 1997 may seem an odd year to be exposing the need for radical reengineering of bank costs and pricing.

Record earnings have been achieved by U.S. banks in 1992–1996.[1] The asset quality difficulties of the 1980s and the early 1990s (first, defaults on lesser developing country debt; second, write-offs of real-estate and highly leveraged transaction loans) have been largely resolved. Deposit interest rates are at their lowest level in decades, loan growth has been strong for three years, and bank spreads are still at historical highs. Bankers, therefore, might well respond: "Why worry? Be happy." They are not viewing bank process redesign as the crux of long-term survival and success.

These favorable conditions should be viewed as a breathing space, during which time unsustainable, supernormal profits can be used to fund the one-time charges associated with reengineering. The industry cannot afford its cost base, nor can it afford to continue underpricing for the value being provided to its customers.

Bank costs are analogous to a pot of overcooked, tangled spaghetti. Complex interdependencies between ill-designed processes and

---

1   Bank Securities Monthly, SNL Securities, February 1997.

marketing approaches create a daunting organizational challenge. Customers have recognized this and are growing to prefer freshly designed products from specialist suppliers, which provide superior service value at lower cost (for example, telephone-based suppliers like Midland Direct and Royal Bank's Direct Line, captive finance companies such as GMAC, mutual fund suppliers such as Fidelity, commercial paper underwriters, and mortgage banks).

The banking industry nonetheless does have significant competitive advantages with which to counter this trend: superior credit underwriting skills; control of the payment systems (at least for the time being); powerful branch and sales-force distribution networks; and unique franchises that are the result of high, current customer inertia. However, bankers need to leverage these advantages through new, customer-focused, streamlined, and redesigned services to their markets, and they should make customers pay for the value being provided. This situation is the result of a complicated evolution over three distinct competitive eras:

1. 1960–1981—The rule of regulated oligopolies.
2. 1981–1990—The rise of disintermediation and excess credit risk.
3. 1990s—The reengineering imperative.

Although my focus in this chapter will be U.S. banks, many of the observations apply equally to banks worldwide.

ERA 1: 1960–1981–THE RULE OF REGULATED OLIGOPOLIES

Geographic and price regulation in the 1960s and 1970s led to a fragmented, localized and geographically dispersed banking industry. The top five competitors controlled only about 5 percent of consumer deposits, retail credit and mortgages. Even for larger corporate customers, where competition did become national, they controlled only about 20 percent of total commercial and industrial (C&I) loans and commercial paper. In contrast, the top five car manufacturers controlled over 95 percent of their market.

Regulatory constraints led to oligarchic, cartel-like pricing. Competition was often fierce, but it was generally based on giveaway services that bankers and customers alike saw and priced as bundled. Take retail product pricing, for example. Customers and banks knew that when interest rates were high the wide spreads from cheap core deposits would compensate

FIGURE 1.1

The Contracyclical Returns of Retail Deposits and Credits
Contribution—$Billions

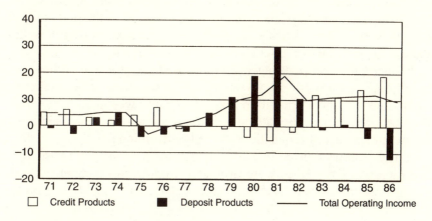

Source: Board of Governors of the Federal Reserve System.

for, or subsidize, thinner credit returns. Conversely, when interest rates were low, wide credit spreads would offset the reduced deposit subsidy. Figure 1.1 illustrates the contracyclical operating income of deposit and credit products from the branch-based retail and commercial markets.

In general, returns were attractive, and bankers were prepared to accept cross-subsidies between the two sides of the balance sheet over the course of the interest rate cycle. Indeed, the general trend of total earnings was upward through 1981, as interest rates rose. The gross deposit subsidy from individual and small commercial customers increased from $12 billion in 1977 to $63 billion in 1981. The 1981 subsidy allowed bankers to absorb the negative credit spread of $9 billion for retail loans that usury laws caused that year. Moreover, given the size of the deposit subsidy, the total operating expense base of the branches seemed insignificant, at about $38 billion; banks expanded their networks, therefore, opening an additional 16,800 branches between 1960 and 1980, for a total of 37,016 branches in the United States.

Similarly, in the wholesale market, the spread over prime for medium-term, floating-rate loans to top corporate borrowers was about 100 basis points (as opposed to about 30–40 basis points in the mid-1990s) and corporate demand deposits as a percentage of loans were about 30 percent (as opposed to about 5 percent in the mid-1990s). The latter excess balances reflected the limited cash management focus of most corporate treasurers, and their willingness to pay their "house bankers" compensating balances, rather than transaction-specific fees, on a bundled relationship basis. There were no alternative suppliers (except at the long end of the bond market), and the wholesale market was a comfortable social arena of golf outings and other sporting events. Banks could afford high-cost marketing through traditional relationship managers and still produce attractive returns.

Competition was on a very localized basis. Interstate consolidation was prohibited, and, even within states, few banks were dominant players. This was due either to state unit banking laws or to the inability of competitors to afford acquisitions of well-performing peers.

The industry existed in a cosy regulatory cocoon where costs could rise rapidly, as revenues were protected by law and competitive self-interest. As a result, bank staff grew from 1.0 million in 1970 to 1.5 million in 1980.[2]

ERA 2: 1981–1991–THE RISE OF DISINTERMEDIATION AND EXCESS CREDIT RISK

The U.S. financial world changed with the Depository Institutions Deregulation and Monetary Control Act of 1980. The competitive playing field was fundamentally altered both legally, by admitting "dumb" savings and loan entry to bank liability and credit markets and, de facto, by the dynamics of disintermediation of deposits and commercial assets, and the crumbling of intrastate and interstate barriers to consolidation. The Regulation Q rate ceiling was removed. The impacts on the retail (consumer and small business) market, the commercial banking business, and the overall bank will be examined in turn.

The Retail Banking Challenge

Beginning in 1981 the U.S. banking industry experienced a fundamental repricing and a radical change in the competitive dynamics for core deposit products. The net interest margin from retail and commercial deposits fell

---

2   *Survey of Current Business,* March 1985, March 1986, January 1992; *Statistical Abstract of the United States 1993, 113th Edition,* U.S. Department of Commerce, Economics and Statistics Administration, Bureau of the Census.

FIGURE 1.2

Money Market Mutual Funds

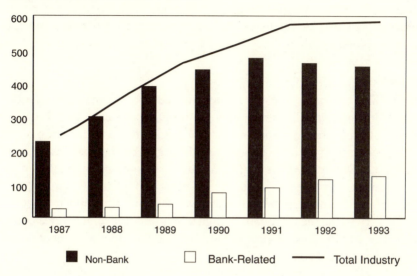

Source: Lipper Analytical Services, Inc.

from $63 billion in 1981 to about $27 billion in 1986, for example, as average spreads on consumer deposits fell from 750 to 180 basis points. Reflecting this change, operating income from consumer and small commercial liabilities fell from $40 billion to a loss of $4 billion. This was caused by a basic shift to interest rate-sensitive products, which increased from 73 percent to 86 percent of bank deposits between 1980 and 1990,[3] largely in response to the disintermediation opportunity for deposits presented by new-entrant competition such as money market mutual funds. Figure 1.2 shows the rise of these funds between 1987 and 1993.

Such product alternatives for bank customers' basic liquidity accounts were accompanied by opportunities readily to convert traditional savings balances to well-diversified stock and bond mutual funds, and to new insurance products (universal and variable life policies), that were primarily investment vehicles.

At the same time, two trends appeared in retail credit markets: the movement toward national product competition among banks and the emergence of fierce non-bank competitors.

---

3   *Statistical Abstract, 113th Edition*

National Product Players

Economies of scale in processing, credit scoring information, and national advertising led to an inevitable squeeze on the local consumer credit supplier. Between 1980 and 1990, for example, the top 10 bank mortgage servicers increased their share from 4 to 8 percent of total servicing.[4]

Non-Bank Competitors

Meanwhile, non-bank competitors began to eat the consumer bank lender's lunch. Non-bank credit cards, such as the Discover card and the AT&T Universal card, grew outstandings to $11.3 billion and $3.8 billion respectively, becoming the third- and thirteenth-largest card portfolios by 1990.[5] Between 1987 and the first quarter of 1993 the commercial banks' market share among the top 25 credit card issuers fell from 89 percent to 64 percent.[6] This non-bank penetration has, of course, continued since (see Figure 1.3). In the meantime, mortgage banks and financial service companies, such as GE Credit Corporation, became formidable competitors for origination and servicing.

Despite these pressures on both the core liability and the core asset products in their retail markets, bankers failed to unbundle their service package to consumers and small business owners, and to price accordingly. They continued to focus on spread income instead of pricing to the perceived value of individual services and transactions. Fee income grew, but in a haphazard way, based on cost-plus or competitor-matching pricing approaches. Costs continued to grow, with bank staff remaining at about 1.5 million from 1980 to 1990 (even though a total of $88 billion had been spent on new technology) and with the number of bank branches increasing from 37,016 to 54,126.[7]

The Commercial Banking Challenge

During the 1980s both demand and supply factors radically changed the bank intermediation role for wholesale customers.

---

4   *American Banker*, May 19, 1981; October 16, 1990.

5   *American Banker Top Numbers 1990; Ranking the Banks, Top Numbers 1992 Edition,* American Banker.

6   *Ranking the Banks, Top Numbers, 1992 Edition,* American Banker.

7   *Statistical Abstract, 113th Edition*

FIGURE 1.3

Non-Bank Credit Card Penetration

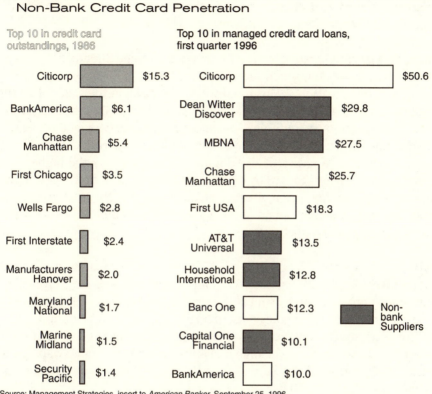

Top 10 in credit card outstandings, 1986

Citicorp	$15.3
BankAmerica	$6.1
Chase Manhattan	$5.4
First Chicago	$3.5
Wells Fargo	$2.8
First Interstate	$2.4
Manufacturers Hanover	$2.0
Maryland National	$1.7
Marine Midland	$1.5
Security Pacific	$1.4

Top 10 in managed credit card loans, first quarter 1996

Citicorp	$50.6
Dean Witter Discover	$29.8
MBNA	$27.5
Chase Manhattan	$25.7
First USA	$18.3
AT&T Universal	$13.5
Household International	$12.8
Banc One	$12.3
Capital One Financial	$10.1
BankAmerica	$10.0

Non-bank Suppliers

Source: Management Strategies, insert to *American Banker,* September 25, 1996.

Demand Factors

Commercial borrowers became more sophisticated than ever before. In the large corporate market and the upper middle commercial market, borrowers negotiated each transaction separately and investigated alternatives to bank funding, rather than maintaining a loyal relationship with a house banker.

As a result, the commercial banker's role as a provider of funds to the corporate market changed. Commercial banks traditionally provided short- and medium-term loans to borrowers in all classes of risk, leaving longer-term equity and debt funding to investment banks. By the mid-1980s, changes in demand patterns reduced the commercial banks' virtual monopoly on short-term and medium-term liquidity financing, essentially limiting them to a role of risk-based lending at the shakier end of the market. As early as 1982, Goldman Sachs was providing as much financing to large corporations as Citibank.

Short-Term Financing. Better credits turned directly to the commercial paper market which increased from $124 billion to $548 billion between 1980 and 1992.[8] This trend was a reflection of the superior credit ratings of prominent corporations, which gave them a short-term cost-of-funds advantage over traditional commercial bank lenders, and increased market liquidity deriving from the deregulation and internationalization of capital markets. In turn, this development was driven by the higher-risk profile of large banks caused by developing country debt, highly leveraged transaction financing, and real-estate credit exposures. By 1993, therefore, only Morgan Guaranty retained an AAA rating,[9] and commercial paper enjoyed a distinct price advantage.

Medium-Term Financing Similar disintermediation resulted when investment banks in both the domestic market and the Euromarket introduced products such as medium-term notes. Between 1981 and 1992 intermediate Eurodollar notes outstanding increased from $2 billion to $80 billion.[10] Moreover, the growth of the swap markets facilitated an indirect access to these products for higher-risk names. Interest rate swaps grew from $170.1 billion in 1985 to $4.6 trillion in 1993 at an average compound growth rate of 60 percent per annum.[11]

Long-Term Financing Last, the growth in junk bonds issued by investment banks provided weaker companies access to the long end of the capital markets. Between 1980 and 1990 the junk market expanded from $30 billion to $226 billion. Even though the market reversed in 1990 and 1991, it bounced back with new offerings of $33 billion in 1992 and $55 billion in 1993 (see Figure 1.4).[12]

Moreover, the market's appetite for traditional equity and bond issues enabled corporations to restructure their balance sheets—by more than $1 trillion in 1993 new issues alone.

---

8   Ibid.

9   Neil Godsey of SNL Securities, November 1993.

10   *Euromoney*, September 1993.

11   *Euromoney*, April 1993; Pen Pendleton of DeWe Rogerson Company.

12   Goldman Sachs; Drexel Burnham Lambert; Securities Data Company, Inc.

FIGURE 1.4

Annual High-Yield Debt Offerings

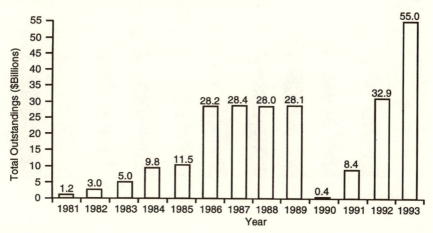

Source: Goldman Sachs

Overall, changes in demand patterns led to a redefinition of the banks' commercial credit role from a virtual monopoly of credit origination across all maturities in the 1970s to a shorter-term role with riskier names in the 1990s.

Supply Factors

Even as demand for commercial loans diminished, suppliers grew in number and shifted in their relationships with each other. Regulatory changes helped to create a situation in which banks found their margins squeezed by an increased cost of funds and declining loan yields. This occurred because both banks and new entrant competitors underpriced, either because they did not understand borrower risk or because they wanted to gain market share.

Increased Cost of Funds   The removal of Regulation Q and other deposit-pricing controls led to a dramatic increase in U.S. bank funding costs. Between 1979 and 1992 the spread between one-year Treasuries and the weighted cost of funds for U.S. commercial banks decreased from 419 basis points to 91 basis points.[13]

---

13   *Federal Reserve Bulletin*, July 1993.

FIGURE 1.5

Commercial Banks' Net Interest Margin by Net Charge-Off
Rate-Deciles

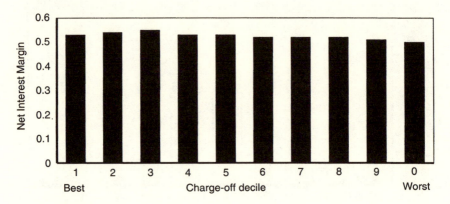

Source: Federal Reserve.

Weak Bank Pricing.   Many commercial banks failed to charge for
the risks that they were undertaking. Figure 1.5 shows that the net interest
margins earned by the worst charge-off performers in 1986 in no way
reflected the riskiness of their portfolios.[14]

The Loan Pricing Corporation of New York has estimated that a
B-rated small business borrower would have to pay almost 2.5 percent over
cost of funds just to cover historical losses. In fact, the average yield has
been 3.0 to 3.5 percent, leaving only 50 to 100 basis points to cover
marketing, credit, loan administration and branch servicing costs, and
contribution to overhead, let alone a return to shareholders. How did this
happen?

Many players failed to understand the marginal costs that needed to
be covered by commercial loan prices for three principal reasons. First,
many weak players viewed their average cost of deposits as their funding
cost, ignoring both the implicit asset and liability mismatching risk that this
entailed, and the cross-subsidy of their lending business by the deposit base
that this involved. Second, they ignored noncash costs, particularly the
required return on equity (ROE), that the incremental loan necessitated.

---

14   Federal Reserve.

Last, many either did not know which marketing, administration and other direct costs were associated with commercial lending, or treated them as fixed costs.

It was hard to compete with players who priced a loan at an 8 percent interest rate, thinking that their costs were only the weighted average cost of deposits of 4 percent, when in fact:

- ◆ The matched debt-funding costs were, perhaps, 6 percent.
- ◆ Noncash funding costs for required returns on capital, Federal Deposit Insurance Corporation (FDIC) insurance and reserve requirements were an additional 1.4 percent.
- ◆ Projectable loan losses amounted to 25–70 basis points.
- ◆ Marketing, credit, and administrative costs required a further 70–80 basis points. Pricing at 9 percent to cover marginal costs (let alone make a contribution to overhead) against competitors priced at 8 percent was simply impossible.

Moreover, competition led to a trickle-down impact throughout the wholesale market, with smaller companies negotiating thinner margins. Figure 1.6, for example, illustrates the ability of smaller companies to achieve money market-based pricing of loans. Even at the $125–$250 million sales range, 45 percent of borrowers in 1988 were able to avoid prime rate–based loans.

New Entrant Competition   Foreign banks were simultaneously recognizing that their lower cost of capital gave them an advantage to undercut U.S. bank pricing. Although pre-Basel[15] capital requirements and associated required returns on capital for Japanese, French, German, and other foreign banks can be debated, it could be estimated that a Japanese bank, for example, had a cost-of-funds advantage of as much as 80 to 90 basis points in the 1980s. It is not surprising, therefore, that the share of U.S. commercial loans held by foreign banks increased from 33 percent in 1981 to 42 percent by 1992 (including their offshore branches and agencies).

---

15   The Basel Agreement was signed at the Bank for International Settlement (BIS) in Basel,
       Switzerland in July 1988 by central bank representatives from the Group of 10 countries
       (Belgium, Canada, France, Germany, Italy, Japan, the Netherlands, Sweden, Switzerland,
       the United Kingdom and the United States) and from Luxembourg, providing the historical
       setting for the current risk-based capital adequacy standards. (Source: *Encyclopedia of
       Banking and Finance.*)

FIGURE 1.6

Money Market–Based Loan Rates by Corporate Sales
Classes, 1988

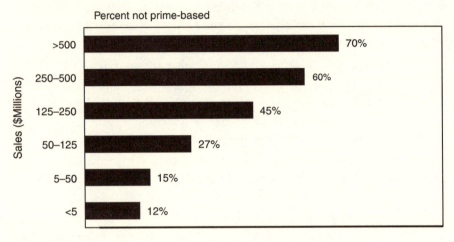

Percent not prime-based

Source: Federal Reserve.

Moreover, the removal of regulatory barriers to commercial lending
by savings institutions led to an increase in commercial loans held by
savings and loan (S&L) associations—from $5 billion in March 1984 to
$25 billion by March 1988. The presence of federal deposit insurance
simultaneously subverted market controls on capacity by implicitly subsi-
dizing the cost of deposits. This allowed weak thrifts to bid up interest
rate-sensitive deposits further in order to fund the cash flow drain caused
by their nonperforming loans and operating losses. The 28 percent of thrifts
that were clearly insolvent in January 1987, for example, continued to raise
$51 billion in deposits between then and June 1988. This enabled them to
fund their nonperforming loans and originate new debt. Although this
source of "dumb" capacity has been removed by the S&L crisis and by the
Federal Deposit Insurance Corporation Improvement Act of 1991, the
legacy of foreign bank and S&L competition on pricing persists.

Non-Bank Commercial Lending   Non-bank lenders, such as
insurance companies and finance companies, became increasingly aggressive in lending to commercial borrowers. Finance companies alone held

over $375 billion in 1995 or 51 percent of total C&I loans,[16] compared with $234 billion or 39 percent in 1988.[17] Although the threat has existed for well over a decade, bankers are only beginning to realize the likely long-term impact that this shift will have on their small business lending.

Overregulation, the deterioration of the bank funding cost advantage, securitization and changes in customer behavior are the main trends leading to the shift that is taking place. In addition, as Harrison Young, the FDIC's former director of resolutions, has stated, "Gone are the days when a bank could offset thin-margin products with other more costly services to the same customer. Today customers take their business to whatever company offers the best price."[18]

Suppliers' trade credits are also a major source of funds for small businesses, and small finance companies are a growing competitive threat in specific regions. In addition, non-bank Small Business Administration (SBA) lenders, such as The Money Store, and leasing companies also have a significant presence. Proposals in the U.S. Congress to create a secondary market in small business loans could make the non-bank threat even more formidable. Legislation has been reintroduced to create a market for securitized small business loans backed by government guarantees.

Earnings Impact
There has been a significant earnings impact from such reduction in demand for, and increase in supply of, traditional bank loans. Between 1980 and 1992 the spread over prime for medium-term, floating-rate loans to top corporate borrowers declined from about 100 basis points to roughly between 30 and 40 basis points. Moreover, "relationship returns" that might have cross-subsidized the lost spread (from traditional compensating balances, cash management services, and nonasset trade and service products) were simultaneously decimated. Between the early 1970s and the 1980s, for example, demand deposits as a percentage of loans in the large corporate market declined from about 30 percent to about 5 percent.

16   *Federal Reserve Bulletin,* September 1996.
17   *Federal Reserve Bulletin,* July 1993.
18   *American Banker*, October 1, 1993.

Bankers' Response to the Challenge

In many ways, bankers responded to the challenges of the second era as though they were in a time warp. Rather than addressing the fundamental mismatch of their costs with the new competitive and regulatory environment, they embarked on a binge of high-risk lending. ("If we have high costs, we had better seek high-yield loans to cover them.") In addition, their attention was diverted to geographic expansion and the latest technological or product fads. They continued to fail to unbundle products and price to value. Their response to meeting the true economic challenges was, at best, half-hearted and did not address the core cost and pricing issues.

Credit Risk Binge

To meet the margin squeeze on traditional commercial lending, bankers took a higher-risk profile in their loan portfolio to achieve required returns. Domestic commercial real-estate lending increased from 16 percent to 22 percent of loans between 1985 and 1990. The price, as with lesser-developed country debt and loans in highly leveraged transactions, did not adjust for the risk undertaken and resulted in another write-off debacle—$108 billion between 1990 and 1992.[19]

Geographic Consolidation

From 1980 to 1995 the number of U.S. banks declined from 14,435 to below 9,900.[20] The motivation for such consolidation was to gain economies of scale and market dominance. But these objectives often proved hard to achieve in practice (largely because of ineffective integration rather than the intrinsic economic potential of consolidation). Moreover, acquisitions often diverted management attention from addressing the inefficiencies of their core bank, at an incalculable cost.

Product Proliferation

Banking changed from a simple intermediation business (raise deposits/make loans) into a complex financial supermarket with many "flavor-of-the-month" specials. In light of geographic expansion, such product

---

19   Analysis based on data received from Ferguson & Company, June 1993.

20   *Statistical Abstract, 113th Edition.*

FIGURE 1.7

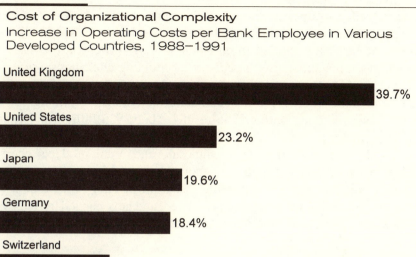

Cost of Organizational Complexity
Increase in Operating Costs per Bank Employee in Various
Developed Countries, 1988–1991

United Kingdom
39.7%

United States
23.2%

Japan
19.6%

Germany
18.4%

Switzerland
12.1%

Source: Solomon Brothers.

complexity led to incredible challenges for process management. Parallel systems and functions were created in unintegrated (or "underintegrated") affiliates. Program code was adulterated to meet new product needs. Organization complexity increased as matrix management was installed for lines of business, products, and geographies. And new strategic investments were often supplements to, rather than replacements for, existing infrastructure.

This all led to an increase in operating costs per bank employee in the U.S. of 23 percent between 1988 and 1991.[21] (Incidentally, as Figure 1.7 shows, this phenomenon was not only a U.S. problem. Salomon Brothers stated in a review of 50 leading banks in 11 countries, "Weak product management skills, the undertaking of ambitious blockbuster projects and the continuing evolution of technology have caused . . . a significant but unquantifiable waste of human and financial resources."[22])

---

21   *Cost Management in Global Banking*, Salomon Brothers, October 1993.

22   Ibid

Pricing Inadequacies

Bankers failed to upgrade their pricing approaches for transaction services, geographic differentiation and commercial loans (on a risk-adjusted basis). At best, they shifted to cost-plus pricing—often on the basis of meaningless, manufacturing-based, cost accounting allocations—or competitor-matching pricing. They failed to look outward to their customers' perceived value and risk profiles, and their relative market pricing power, as the basis for price setting. The result? About $30 billion in forgone pretax earnings in 1996.[23]

With their most profitable wholesale and retail products cherry-picked, bankers turned to high-risk lending, geographic expansion forays, and new products to offset reduced core earnings. They failed to address the basic cost and price issues that they faced, and have carried the baggage of their behavior into the third competitive era.

ERA 3: 1990s—THE REENGINEERING IMPERATIVE

Although the years between 1992 and 1996 were banner years for bank profitability, a new challenge is arising that further accentuates the imperative to reengineer. The industry is facing a "revenue crunch."

On the liability side of the balance sheet, the core deposit base is crucially threatened. On the asset side, there is a continuation of a process of gradual obsolescence of banks in the commercial lending arena, combined with increasingly vicious competition for core consumer assets.

The U.S. commercial lending trends have been described earlier in some detail. The phenomenon of core deposit erosion constitutes, however, a further intensification of the economic pressure on U.S. banks as their traditional revenue base is squeezed. Three areas will be considered:

- The cause of supernormal returns.
- The resulting outflow of core deposits.
- The reengineering imperative that unsustainable margins impose.

---

23   Analysis based on data received from Ferguson & Company, February 1997.

The 1992–1996 Return Mirage

Federal Reserve chairman Alan Greenspan's outstanding management of interest rates stabilized the banking industry throughout 1991–1993. He reduced inflationary expectations and steepened the yield curve, allowing banks to arbitrage their short-funding by investing in zero-risk Treasuries. Savers picked up the tab, since high liquidity enabled banks to price deposits at historically low levels. Then Greenspan engineered a "soft landing" of long-term rates.

The net result of this has been four years of historically extraordinary net interest margins. The FDIC reported average spreads 30 to 40 basis points higher than historical norms. These resulted from the combination of loan price "stickiness" as rates fell, the yield curve arbitrage opportunity to short-fund Treasuries, and the aggressive downward repricing and then maintenance of low savings rates. In 1992, this amounted to $15 billion of extraordinary pretax earnings, roughly one-third of the industry total. Only a partial erosion of such supernormal returns occurred in 1993–1996, offset by strong loan growth.

This windfall enabled the industry to stabilize and thrive. As a percentage of bank assets, nonperforming assets and 90-days-past-due loans declined from 3.2 to 1.1 percent between January 1, 1992, and March 31, 1996; net charge-offs to average loans declined from 1.7 to 0.6 percent, while reserves to nonperformers rose from 52 to 159 percent.[24]

The Deposit Crunch

The Federal Reserve, therefore, helped to save the U.S. banking industry through its masterly management of interest rates. There was, however, a price to be paid: savers provided a massive subsidy for the cleanup of banks' problem assets.

During the early 1980s consumers were conditioned to rely on the cash flow associated with high interest rates to fund their day-to-day needs. In the world of 2 to 3 percent savings rates, core customers have been forced to disintermediate from their traditional deposit home–banks.

This merely reflects an acceleration of a long-term trend. In 1983 household time deposits and mutual fund assets amounted to $1.8 trillion,

---

24   *The SNL Quarterly Bank Digest*, July 1996.

with banks holding an 84 percent share. By March 1996 the market had grown to $3.8 trillion, but banks controlled just a little over 32 percent. Banks have been facing the dilemma of "getting on the boat" or losing the funds to outsiders.

Working first with mutual fund companies as third-party providers, then through sales of proprietary funds, and potentially through acquisitions (such as Mellon's purchase of Dreyfus), banks have amassed a significant share of total mutual funds holdings. Even excluding money market funds, banks accounted for 15 percent of long-term mutual funds at December 31, 1995, up from 3 percent at year-end 1992.

It is true that bank funds are still dominated by less interest-sensitive money market funds (more than two-thirds, as estimated by Lipper Analytical Services.) Yet that still leaves $116 billion in equities and $73 billion in fixed-income funds under bank management. Moreover, equity funds accounted for 27 percent of total bank funds in June 1996, growing from 12 percent at the end of 1992.[25]

Why is this trend important? It is not clear that customers understand their exposure to loss of principal from their new investments, no matter how much bank sales personnel insist that they are explaining the risk. A preliminary survey by the Securities and Exchange Commission (SEC) found that an astonishing two-thirds of money market fund purchasers believed the products were federally insured. Although these figures are for all fund purchasers, not merely bank customers, the SEC also found that 30 percent of the latter believed all mutual funds sold by banks—even stock and bond funds—were federally insured.

In just 15 years, from 1980 through 1995, the number of U.S. households owning mutual funds jumped from 6 percent to 31 percent. This is causing a radical realignment of household balance sheets. The Federal Reserve Board's survey of consumer finances[26] showed that, between 1989 and 1992, consumers increased the share of their financial assets in long-term mutual funds from 10 percent to 13 percent, whereas their holdings of deposits and money funds fell from 37 percent to 31 percent. Significantly, the increase in share was most heavily concentrated among households in which the principal wage earner of the household was between 55 and 64

---

25   Lipper Analytical Service, *American Banker.*

26   *Federal Reserve Bulletin*, November 1993.

TABLE 1.1

New versus Seasoned Mutual Fund Investor Profile, 1993

	Average per Household	
	New	**Seasoned**
Financial assets*	$60,000	$121,000
Mutual fund investments	$21,000	$45,000
Median age (years)	37	46
Median household income	$40,000	$50,000

*Excluding real estate and assets in employer-sponsored retirement funds.

years of age. Moreover, the profile of new purchasers is far different from that of more seasoned investors, as shown in Table 1.1.[27]

The significance of the deposit disintermediation of relatively unsophisticated bank customers is that it may threaten one of the most critical sources of banks' competitive advantage and revenue potential: customer inertia. More than 60 percent of consumer relationships with banks exceed 10 years, and 50 percent of family business owners with sales less than $5 million have similar loyalty to their banks.

These relatively unsophisticated customers have always relied on the protection of principal (legally, through FDIC insurance and, de facto, in bank failures). In chasing bond and stock fund yields, customers have implicitly—not consciously—taken on market and principal risk.

When rates rise, bond fund principal will be lost and, at some point, equity markets will drop from existing high valuations. When that time comes, there are going to be many angry bank consumers and small business owners. These investors are a different type of investors from traditional mutual fund purchasers, being more reliant on cash flow from their savings. The potential will then be extremely high for political intervention for the regulation of bank mutual fund activities to protect the retirement funds of voters. The banks will also face the loss of their most attractive and most loyal customers.

---

27   *Bank Management*, October 1993.

Not only the core revenue base of stable deposit earnings is threatened (unless one believes balances will return to traditional bank deposits during a market downturn, which is highly questionable), but also the central source of loyal bank relationships with their customers.

The Reengineering Imperative

Current loan growth and interest margins cannot last forever. Economic growth may exceed expectations, thereby fuelling inflation. Loan pricing will continue to adjust downward over time, and either securities gains have already been realized or holdings will roll over and reprice at much lower yields.

It is not clear that continued loan growth will fill the revenue void. Many bankers say that they will continue to grow their assets to save the day. Loan demand has driven returns in the last two years, but the structural barriers to profitable lending and intense non-bank competition (in what are already overcapacity markets) will make sustained "growing into the cost base" through even more loans highly unlikely.

Lower spreads and flattening loan growth will again exert pressure on bank profitability, primarily because banks' operating costs are too high and their prices are too low. The average efficiency ratio (costs to revenues) for publicly traded banks has remained at about 65 percent since the mid-1980s—after adjusting it for the mid-1990s supernormal spreads. However, top-quartile banks are operating with efficiency ratios in the range of 50 to 55 percent.[28]

Banks have systematically underpriced their products and services. When prices and services are broken down and the perceived value of transactions to different classes of customers is analyzed in detail, banks can increase their noninterest revenues by 15 to 20 percent with little or no account runoff. Customers simply value bank services more than bankers think.

The crux of the reengineering imperative is that, collectively, the emerging deposit disintermediation, a narrowing of spreads, the likely flattening of loan demand, and an unsustainable cost/pricing structure will collectively create a "revenue crunch" for traditional income streams.

---

28   Analysis based on data received from SNL Securities and Ferguson & Company,
       June 1996.

CHAPTER 2

The Cost Impact of the Past

INTRODUCTION

Given the magnitude of change that the U.S. banking industry has undergone since 1980, it is not surprising that the cost structure of banks is characterized by duplicative and redundant activities, onerous and hierarchical management structures, dual and triple controls, and other vestiges of the past.

To illustrate, consider the following situation that arose at a bank in London. (See Figure 2.1). A consolidation of multiple buildings constructed more than 100 years ago had transformed the bank into a rabbit warren of offices. Getting from point A to point B was never easy. Mail and packages were delivered to the front entrance of the bank and handed over to the mailroom staff. Upon receipt, a messenger would carry a package up one flight of stairs and past 10 or so senior executive offices on the second floor; would stop to chat with fellow staff and deliver other mail along the way; and then would descend a second flight of stairs, enter a small room, and place the package in an electronic device to x-ray it for bombs! Redesigning the task so that the messenger simply walked around the exterior of the building and entered through the rear door saved the bank $30,000 annually.

Although this was obviously an extreme case of a misdesigned task, it is far from unique, as the following further illustrations show: A bank in the Northeast had appointed a new chief executive officer (CEO) to one of its mid-sized subsidiary banks. To acquaint himself with the bank's business and functions, he requested a presentation from each line-of-business

FIGURE 2.1

The Package Deliverer

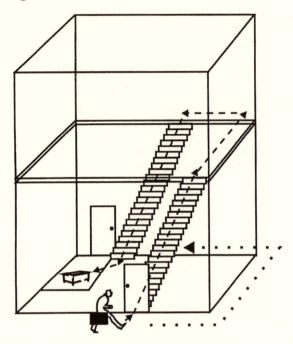

manager and functional head, detailing his or her department's economics, strategy, organization, staff skills and so on. Each report contained approximately 150 pages. Three years later the CEO was astounded to discover that these reports were still being produced "just in case" he ever asked to see one again— at an annual cost of more than $250,000 to the bank.

A superior-performing bank in the Midwest employed nine people full-time to verify the signature on every check it processed. The rationale behind this task was that comprehensive verification would decrease the risk of negligence suits. Despite several instances of forgery, however, the verification group had not identified a single fraudulent item, nor taken part in any legal defense, for at least five years (when records began). Establishing verification of checks only above $20,000 reduced the staff by 67 percent, saved the bank $50,000 annually, and led to two forgeries being identified.

In a large Southeastern bank, middle managers had, on average, only three direct reports and there were in some instances 18 layers of management (excluding operations) between the CEO and the customer. Increasing the number of reports, and thereby reducing the number of management layers, not only led to a savings of $650,000 per annum but also increased the customer focus of the bank.

A regional credit card issuer was contemplating whether to install a new automated decision-making system after a positive response from a direct mail campaign overwhelmed its processing capacity. The investment in a new system, however, became unnecessary when it was realized that the parameters of the review process had been set so narrowly that almost 90 percent of applications were being flagged for manual review. The real bottleneck had been not the existing automation but rather the number of people required to manually review the sudden influx of applications. By adjusting exceptions rules, the bank was able to save $60,000 annually and improve turnaround time.

A regional mortgage unit was responsible for gathering the customer information needed for underwriting. An investigation into the mortgage office's enormous postage costs discovered that the parent bank's in-house courier service invariably arrived in the morning even though the customer files were not ready until the evening. This forced the office to use an overnight delivery service, which picked up the unit's mail at 5:00 PM. The office essentially circumvented the bank's delivery system and created its own. By rescheduling the courier and imposing strict guidelines for the use of outside delivery services, postage expenses were cut by 25 percent per annum.

Most bankers reading this book will be able to cite similar examples of unnecessary bureaucratic processes, tasks, and systems. The cost problem goes much deeper, however, than such anecdotes. Banks' approaches to their customers, their products, and their geographic markets have been systematically misdesigned. The same is true of the processes, functions, physical plants, and systems that serve the banks. In total, it is estimated that this pervasive obsolescence constitutes an annual pretax earnings opportunity of $30 billion for the U.S. banking industry— the cost reengineering opportunity. This amounts to 35–40 percent of the total pretax profits of U.S. banks in 1996.[1]

How did redundancy, duplication, bureaucratic burden, and organizational complexity of this magnitude come about? Part of the reason is the level and increasing acceleration of change that the industry has faced.

---

1   Analysis of data retrieved from Ferguson & Company, February 1997

Practices, processes, and systems developed between 1930 and 1980 were fixed with "bandaids" to meet changing competitive and regulatory conditions, when major surgery was required. New cost structures were created that supplemented, rather than substituted, the structures of the past. Increasing geographic and product reach led to the creation of complicated matrix management organizations supposedly to control and integrate the ever more complex infrastructure of banks.

Overshadowing these explanations, however, is the fact that cost levers within the banking industry are wholly different from those of manufacturing companies. Banks have considerably more interdependencies among their functions, processes, physical plants, and systems than do manufacturing companies producing widgets. Moreover, bank costs are often "common" to multiple customer segments, product families, and geographic regions. (This means that costs are not unique to a particular product, as in a dedicated production line in a manufacturing plant; but shared by multiple products, as in the case of bank back-office data centers.) The following characteristics of bank costs should be considered:

- ◆ Interdependencies of common cost structures.
- ◆ The historical context.
- ◆ The mysteries of bank cost accounting.
- ◆ The response to existing cost structures.

INTERDEPENDENCIES OF COMMON COST STRUCTURES

Figure 2.2 is a very complex chart. In fact, it would need to be three-dimensional to truly capture the levels of interdependencies that exist among and across what I term the "infrastructure levers" and "management levers" (both strategic and organizational) of bank costs.

In their book, *Reengineering the Corporation*,[2] Michael Hammer and James Champy define reengineering as:

> The fundamental rethinking and radical redesign of business processes to achieve dramatic improvements in critical, contemporary measures of performance, such as cost, quality, service and speed.

---

2   Michael Hammer and James Champy, *Reengineering the Corporation*, HarperCollins, Harper Business Press, 1993.

FIGURE 2.2

The Reengineering Levers of Banking

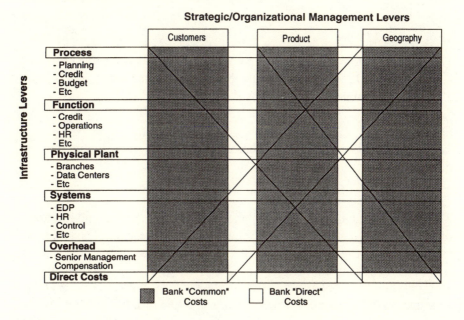

They further define a "process" as "a collection of activities that takes one or more kinds of input and creates an output that is of value to the customer."

Although the authors' refocusing of redesign from tasks to processes is a quantum leap in management theory, the situation in banks is even more complex than the situations they describe for manufacturing firms, explaining why Figure 2.2 is so complicated. Even without the dramatic changes in the industry which have taken place since the mid-1980s, banking has an inherently more complex cost structure than most businesses; costs cannot be linked to a specific product bought by a specific customer in a specific geographic location. The direct, identifiable expenses associated uniquely with any of these three management variables are 5–10 percent of total cost, at most. National product businesses, such as credit cards, are clearly exceptions, not the rule. Rather, most infrastructure levers are common to multiple segment, product, and geographic management levers.

Management Levers

There are three levers of strategic and organizational management: customer, product, and geography.

Customer
The distinct customer segments served by the bank, such as large corporate and middle wholesale markets, small businesses, affluent consumers, middle market consumers, and mass market consumers.

Product
The range of balance- and non-balance-related credit, investment, transaction, and information services provided to customers.

Geographic
The distribution channels (such as branch networks, ATMs, and mortgage offices) and the distributed sales forces, service representatives, and processing staff that cater to the product needs of the various customer segments. Although these may appear to be discrete management levers of cost, they are seldom so in practice. A wholesale banking customer's CEO, for example, is served not only by the wholesale line of business, but also by private bankers and trust officers for personal investments; by branches and ATMs near his or her home and office for cash access and problem resolution; and by the bank's mortgage, auto loan, and credit card companies for personal financing needs.

Infrastructure Levers

There are five levers of cost that are common to all lines of business and organization structures in banks.

Process
In line with Hammer and Champy's definition, a *bank process* is a series of activities or tasks that are inputs leading to a defined output. Examples include credit processes, purchasing, budgeting, and strategic planning. These processes, however, do not consist of disaggregated tasks performed by specialists. Rather, they have different impacts on the multiple customer, the product, and the geographic levers. The staff that serves customers in

banks tends to spend a fraction of its time at various points of the day, month or year on the demands of each process.

Functions

Bank functions, such as credit, finance, human resources, and treasury, more closely resemble the Hammer and Champy model. Organizationally, they are distinct and separate units whose processes (such as accounts payable in finance, and overall portfolio management and credit policy design in credit) are broken into specialized tasks within the functional unit and aggregated into an internal process flow.

Physical Plant

Two obvious examples of common physical plant costs are branch networks and the back-office infrastructure of banks. As many institutions have found, allocated costs do not disappear—although revenues do—when a particular product or customer segment is exited, or when a branch is closed. The size of the mainframe computer, for example, cannot be reduced to reflect the processing time that was necessary (in theory) to serve the customers of a closed branch. In practice, much of the branch's cost will often be transferred to the consolidated location in order to service the needs of retained customers.

Systems

Most electronic data processing (EDP) systems serve multiple customers and geographies, and even products (as product innovations have often been the result of temporary adjustments to existing software). Included in these systems, however, are non-EDP systems, such as incentive compensation, Community Reinvestment Act monitoring, planning and budgeting, and quality control systems that exist across the bank. Once more, tasks trickle down through the bank's hierarchy to serve each of these systems.

"Pure" Overhead

Successfully managing the complex matrix of cost levers is a challenge. As a result, the cost of employing senior managers and their staffs is overlaid on the total expense picture. It should not be surprising that Figure 2.2 appears indecipherable. Even a bank with the most cost-conscious corporate culture will find its expense structure to be extremely complicated because of the level of interdependencies and interrelationships among the levers of cost.

FIGURE 2.3

Spaghetti Costs

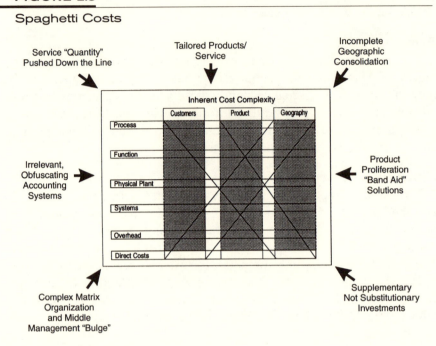

THE HISTORICAL CONTEXT

The banking industry, as discussed, has been weighed down with vestiges of cost structures from past decades. Regulatory protection from market-driven pricing pressures and non-bank competition has created an evolutionary dynamic that has further complicated the cost structure of most banks (summarized in Figure 2.3).

Each line of business and functional area of the bank illustrates how service quantity (rather than quality or value) was pushed down the line because expensive delivery modes were affordable. This was true whether the cost was created to service external customers for retail distribution, retail credit, wholesale, or trust businesses, or to service internal clients for systems and operations, or administrative support.

Geographic expansion and product proliferation subsequently caused an overlay of complexity that further exacerbated the historical cost structure. Moreover, new expenditures on innovative distribution, service, and

FIGURE 2.4

Underlying characteristics of Branch Expenses

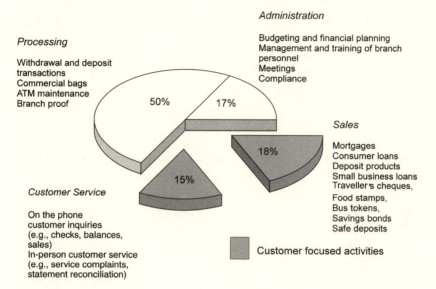

Administration

Budgeting and financial planning
Management and training of branch
personnel
Meetings
Compliance

Processing

Withdrawal and deposit
transactions
Commercial bags
ATM maintenance
Branch proof

50%   17%

Sales

18%   Mortgages
Consumer loans
Deposit products
Small business loans
Traveller's cheques,
Food stamps,
Bus tokens,
Savings bonds
Safe deposits

15%

Customer Service

On the phone
customer inquiries
(e.g., checks, balances,
sales)
In-person customer service
(e.g., service complaints,
statement reconciliation)

Customer focused activities

sales approaches tended to supplement, rather than to substitute for, existing cost structures.

All these factors led to an organizational and hierarchical management structure that reflected not merely the intrinsic complexity of banks but also the aberrations of their historical evolution.

The Regulatory Legacy

The line of business and functional approaches and processes of most banks are a reflection of what was affordable in the past.

Retail Distribution

Figure 2.4 illustrates what I have found time and time again. Customer-related activities in retail branches, such as sales and customer service, constitute, at best, one-third of total branch resource allocations. The majority of branch personnel time is spent on processing and administration. Even customer-related activities are often low-value-added in nature.

Take this example: a platform employee at a branch spent each morning telephoning all customers who were overdrawn the day before. In one instance a customer's account was short by a mere 43 cents. The customer was still called by the employee and an hour later dutifully arrived to deposit exactly 43 cents into his account! Moreover, even when time is spent on sales, it is often on low-value products such as food stamps, bus tokens, and savings bonds.

The predominance of processing and administration activities in branches comes about because it is basic human nature to prefer problem resolution and processing to sales. Helping a customer solve an issue or moving stacks of paper from one side of the desk to the other is inherently satisfying. A customer's gratitude and the physical reassurance of completed paperwork help justify the bank employee's existence and paycheck.

Approaching customers to sell them a product they may not want (or know they want), however, is both embarrassing and ill suited to traditional branch staff skills and personalities.

This pattern has emerged in branches largely as the result of the bundled approach to retail banking for consumers and small business customers that Regulation Q made possible. Because price was set, the differentiating basis of competition was in "giveaway" service quantity—not service quality and value. Because much of the paper arrived at the branches, it was processed there for quick turnaround. If customers had problems, they preferred to speak with people in the branches they knew personally. In the same way, business owners knew the local branch manager from the golf course or other social activities, so the manager was credit-trained to speed up credit decisions.

The fact that all of these tasks formed part of processes including other departments of the bank (handoffs to operations, customer information file management, the credit department), and were inherently inefficient, as well as, in reality, low value, was subsumed by the ability to pay for them through regulated relationship pricing.

Retail Credit

A similar historical impact can be seen in retail credit. An overly complex range of product variations developed, delaying turnaround times. Much of the administrative and processing burden was again pushed down to the front line (often with manual underwriting processes that caused delay), thereby contributing to compliance issues and breaches of standard credit policies. These factors led to inconsistences among geographic regions and redundant dual and triple controls of loan origination and servicing tasks.

Wholesale

Account officers were called "relationship officers" because they were responsible for all interaction with the customer. Again, 50 to 60 percent of their time was spent on administration, whether problem resolution or credit management, instead of on sales. Administrative assistants were, in essence, "gofers," not problem solvers. Credit review and approval and other control processes burgeoned and customers were treated uniformly, with expensive marketers selling the same tailored products to all borrowers. In short, the account officer's time commitment and expense were often disproportionate to the smaller customer's revenue potential. However, in a world of high loan spreads and attractive revenues from compensating balances, unmanaged by corporate treasurers, the luxury of relationship management was not questioned.

Trust

Not surprisingly, similar characteristics were reflected in both the personal and institutional trust businesses. Marketing resources were deployed evenly across profitable and unprofitable, large and small accounts. Trust officers spent much of their time on administration because their service assistants did not contact clients. Each product line was sold by a separate officer to the same customer. Specialized funds management skills were applied to all accounts regardless of their type and size, which increased processing complexity and drove up costs.

Operations

Given the business characteristics summarized above, it is not surprising that functions with an internal client base made service response and empire building a priority over optimal process design. Operations departments tended simply to automate existing manual processes rather than redesign them from scratch. Yet many repetitive processes remained manual because they worked and the controls over them were in place. Nonstandardized product offerings led to process complexity. And processing standards were set to provide the "best" service to all customers rather than tailored to differentiated customer needs.

Technology and Systems

Similarly, technology and systems development projects became bigger and bigger, as users asked for every bell-and-whistle feature and constantly changed their specifications, not understanding the cost that this entailed. Systems staff did not tell users the cost of their requirements because they did not appreciate the need for a cost/benefit justification for development. They gravitated toward single integrated "legacy" systems rather than discrete compatible modules, leading to diseconomies of scale, as miles of code needed reprogramming for minor upgrades. And they adopted a "not-invented-here" mentality with regard to any available packaged or outsourced systems. But the bank could afford it, and most senior management did not understand electronic data processing anyway.

Administration

Superimposed on all this historical baggage were administrative functions (the "glue", to use Hammer and Champy's term) that were faced by the inherently higher complexity of bank costs; the phenomenon of high quantity, decentralized service and processing; and the ability to afford dual and triple controls. Administrative activities consisted of hundreds of small tasks for which no one felt responsible and which no one challenged because each individual task cost too little to bother to change. Moreover, the quid pro quo for regulatory protection was an endless stream of highly repetitive reports. The fact that each report, each control, and each procedure created a trickle-down burden on the bank (and, in aggregate, the cost of controls was inordinately high) slipped through reporting gaps.

Although the legacy of the regulated past has been discussed in the past tense, the fact is that many, if not most, banks are still operating in the same way: servicing and processing are still downstreamed to expensive sales resources. Tailored products are still sold to all customers. Internal constituencies are still served as though response capability should dominate a cost/benefit justification. And the administrative glue that keeps this cost edifice from falling apart is still in place.

GEOGRAPHIC EXPANSION AND PRODUCT PROLIFERATION

As if cost structures were not sufficiently complex, the twin dynamics of bank consolidation and product proliferation have confused them even further.

Bank Consolidation

The still-developing process of bank mergers and acquisitions has added the challenge of managing geographically remote affiliates. This often entails integrating widely differing systems, practices, and cultures from successive acquisitions. From 1980 to 1996 the number of banks declined from 14,435 to around 9,500.[3]

In general, however, bankers have not been particularly successful in integrating their acquisitions. Academic research suggests that larger bank mergers have generally not produced significant cost savings (at least for transactions that did not involve overlapping markets). A study by Aston Associates of 150 acquisitions over a five-year period showed that, on average, savings of only 10 percent of noninterest expense were achieved two years after deal consummation. After adjusting for overall bank cost inflation, even this small improvement was absorbed. As will be discussed in Chapter 4, integration largely fails because too many acquirers lack both the will and the skill to consolidate effectively. Integration results do not reflect the inherent potential for efficiencies of both in-market and interstate transactions.

Part of the reason for this pattern is that the manner in which consolidation has been carried out has given rise to cost diseconomies. Acquired institutions have often retained their legal entity management and support structures, creating the need for a new bureaucracy to buffer contacts between acquirer and acquiree. Parallel, inconsistent processes have required additional staff to translate results and control the newcomer's approaches. Duplication of tasks down the line has burgeoned as affiliate management checks the numbers supplied by the head office and challenges allocations for consolidated operations charges and overhead.

Consider two situations: A Midwestern bank had grown to close to $8 billion in assets through acquisitions in three states. Although it had made significant progress in consolidating data centers, its 14 legal entity affiliates had continued to be managed otherwise as stand-alone banks. Each had a president, a president's office to serve its board of directors, a legal staff, a finance department, human resource managers, and so on. Furthermore,

---

3   *Statistical Abstract of the United States 1995, 117th Edition*, U.S. Department of Commerce, Economics and Statistics Administration, Bureau of the Census.

to ensure responsiveness, the larger affiliates had hoarded their own operations support either to circumvent manually centralized processing or to troubleshoot the "mistakes" of headquarter's staff. In total the hidden cost of this duplication across the system was $15 million, almost 10 percent of the bank's total controllable expense base.

A very large East coast bank had spent several years delayering its senior management from 12 to 3 levels in order to "get closer to its customers." Following a merger of equals, it created a top-level structure of 10 layers in order—a cynic might say—to find slots for most of the senior managers of the two banks.

Such diseconomies are not the inevitable consequence of consolidation, but, in practice, they all too often just seem to occur.

Product Proliferation

Table 2.1 gives an incomplete yet graphic illustration of the number of banking products that have been created since the 1970s. Banks have changed from simple intermediaries, raising savings and demand deposits to lend short or medium-term, into complex financial supermarkets—unfortunately, with too many flavor-of-the-month specials. The implications of this change are threefold.

To Create a Specialist Product Salesforce and Infrastructure?
Banks are constantly tempted to create specialist groups to sell, service, and support new product categories. The problem is that this may create an incremental cost structure for what may prove to be ephemeral demand. Take, for example, the explosion in bank mutual funds. Have bankers created infrastructure at the top of the market that will be hard to dismantle in a downturn? Banks have taken three approaches to selling mutual funds:

- Creating new supplemental costs for a dedicated fund sales force for proprietary funds.
- Selling funds through traditional platform staff.
- Retaining a "variablized" cost structure by selling through the staff of third-party providers.

Each approach has pros and cons. The first maximizes the return from fund sales and keeps a distinct cost structure that can be dismantled (à la brokerage houses) when fund sales decline. The second also gives the full return and can appear to achieve economies of marketing expense through

TABLE 2.1

Corporate and Retail Bank Product Offerings

1970s	1990s	
Non-interest bearing demand deposits	Non-interest-bearing demand deposits	Foreign Exchange (FX) and electronic banking services
Savings accounts	Savings accounts	Foreign exchange options
Certificates of deposit (CDs)	NOW accounts	Domestic funding
Safe deposit box services	Certificates of deposit	Foreign funding
Fixed rate mortgages	IRAs	Multicurrency funding
Student loans	Money market funds	FX forward transactions
Automobile loans	Bond funds	Options
Other installment loans	Equity funds	Securities settlement
Fixed-rate credit cards	Annuities	Securities trading
Revolving credit	Insurance	Receivable financing vehicles
Term loans	Safe deposit box services	Interest rate swaps
Overdrafts	Adjustable rate mortgages	Currency swaps
Letters of credit	Fixed-rate mortgages	Leasing
Domestic funding	Student loans	Securitized assets
Foreign funding	Automobile loans	Employee Stock Ownership Plans (ESOPs)
Securities settlement	Automobile leases	Standby letters of credit
Securities trading	Other installment loans	Account maintenance
Leasing	Fixed-rate credit cards	Account reconciliation
Standby letters of credit	Floating-rate credit cards	Automated clearing house
Account maintenance	Debit cards	Controlled disbursement
Account reconciliation	ATM services	Depository transfer checks
Depository transfer checks	Revolving credit	Direct deposit of payroll
Lock boxes	Term loans	Lock boxes
Money transfer	Overdrafts	Money transfers
Regular disbursements	Letters of credit	Regular disbursements
Bankers acceptances	Asset sales	Zero balance account
International letters of credit	Mergers and acquisitions	Bankers acceptances
Inward/outward document collection	Restructuring	Countertrade advisory
Trade reporting	Leveraged buyouts	Export finance advisory
	Underwriting services	International letters of credit
	Domestic notes and bonds	Inward/outward document collection
	Eurodollar notes and bonds	Trade reporting
	Foreign currency exposure management	

"piggybacking" existing sales resources—but at the expense of complexity in terms of future downsizing. The last gives up part of the return to the third-party supplier but, if the relationship is properly structured, this approach is the easiest to undo. Selecting the right trade-off between return and dedicated, piggybacking, or outsourced infrastructure for new products is a difficult and imperfect science. Whichever choice is made, however, will involve increased cost and complexity.

The Need for Increased Cross-Selling by Marketers

Whether the ultimate sale is by a specialist or generalist, salespeople (and even tellers) are being asked to cross-sell actively an array of investment, credit, information, and transaction products. But this is not easy. The average marketer feels comfortable selling one or, at best, two or three closely related core products. The fear of embarrassment from misdescribing a complicated new offering is high. In addition, gaining a thorough knowledge of any new product involves a considerable commitment of time and energy. If the cross-sell involves a referral to a product specialist, the fear arises that the marketer will sell a poor performance product to one of the referer's best clients, thereby killing the goose that lays the golden eggs.

Merrill Lynch's experience with its innovative Cash Management Account is instructive. It took the admonition of Don Regan, then chairman, to launch the account. Although it was ultimately a highly successful product, brokers simply did not want to risk embarrassment and the potential cannibalization of their client portfolios by selling it. Only a direct threat to bonuses encouraged the marketing of what was, in fact, an easy product to understand and describe. It is, therefore, not difficult to imagine the reluctance of a middle-market lender asked to describe a bank's derivative product capabilities to a customer's chief financial officer (CFO). This need to cross-sell has also involved a new layer of cost in order to: upgrade staff (to compete, for example, with investment banks for experienced corporate finance executives); train salespeople on general consultative sales techniques and specific new product characteristics; and prompt referrals and sales through cash incentives.

The Further Burdening of Systems and Operations

Too frequently, systems and operations have responded to new products with "bandaid" solutions, grafting new product specifications onto already archaic and overburdened software. Marketers have said they needed the new products "now, and at whatever cost." Systems staff have complied, accelerating development cycles (which always exponentially increases cost) and postponing other, often more important, long-term redesign projects.

Supplemental, Not Substitute, Investments

Similar to the impact of product proliferation is the phenomenon of many large-scale bank investment programs leading to a new layer of cost, which supplemented the existing structure rather than replaced it.

U.S. banks have created an infrastructure of more than 120,000 automated teller machines (ATMs) at an estimated capital cost of $8.8 billion (Figure 2.5).[4] The estimated servicing costs of the machines annually is about $2 billion.[5]

Many of the transactions on ATMs are new ones rather than replacements for teller transactions. The number of tellers in the United States has continued to grow since the mid-1980s; tellers per branch have declined, but only to 6.3 and average real dollars of deposits per teller have increased only to about 5.5 million[6] (see Figure 2.6).

Consumers have, in the main, used ATMs to withdraw less money per transaction for security reasons rather than reducing their teller access. This is now beginning to change, but, to date, has not justified electronic delivery on cost displacement. Furthermore, ATM transactions have not displaced checks for payment transactions. Figure 2.7 shows the market share, in billions of dollars, for checks, credit cards, and ATM withdrawals.

We have not moved to a paperless society, and the expected savings in branch staff costs and back-office processing expenses, which were often the justification for the new infrastructure, have not been realized. This is not to say that the value added of the new structures has not been high for customers, helping retention and cross-sales. Any valid justification for the new capital and direct costs should, however, have been from a value and revenue, not a cost-displacement, perspective.

The same is true for much of the technology investment of the last decade. It has been estimated that U.S. banks spent a cumulative total of $88 billion on systems between 1980 and 1990, and such spending is accelerating[7] (Figure 2.8). This may be justified by:

---

4   Data supplied by the Bank Network News Institute.

5   *Statistical Abstract, 113th edition.*

6   *Cost Management in Global Banking*, Salomon Brothers, October 1993.

7   Ibid.

FIGURE 2.5

U.S. ATM Growth, 1973–1995

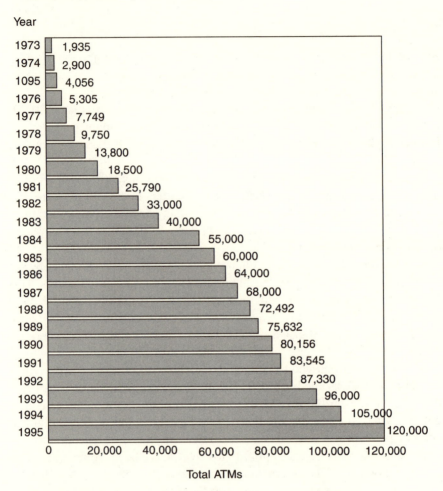

Source: *Nilson Report: Magazine of Bank Administration;* BNN; Speer & Assoc.; *Bank Network News.*

- ◆ The simple need for upgrading to meet capacity constraints.
- ◆ Increasing customer value through ease of access and speed of turnaround.
- ◆ Averting competitive obsolescence versus peers.

FIGURE 2.6

Teller Staffing Levels

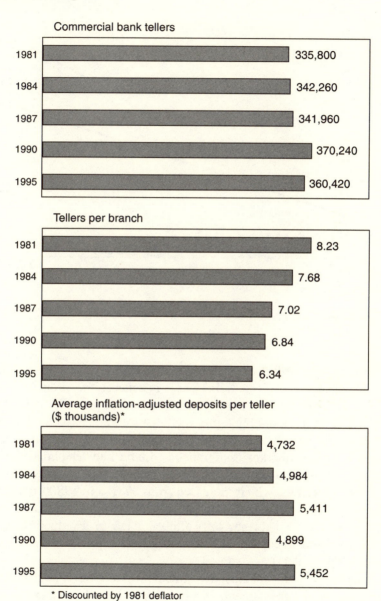

Commercial bank tellers

1981	335,800
1984	342,260
1987	341,960
1990	370,240
1995	360,420

Tellers per branch

1981	8.23
1984	7.68
1987	7.02
1990	6.84
1995	6.34

Average inflation-adjusted deposits per teller
($ thousands)*

1981	4,732
1984	4,984
1987	5,411
1990	4,899
1995	5,452

* Discounted by 1981 deflator

Source: *Monthly Labor Review*, U.S. Department of Labor; *Statistics on Banking*, FDIC.

FIGURE 2.7

U.S. Consumer Payment Systems

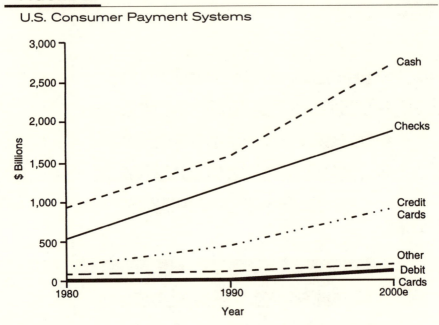

Source: Nilson Report.

Yet, it is far from clear that these investments have displaced existing costs as often projected. In many instances, the proper rationale
should have been the willingness of customers to pay for the increased
value added that technology provided. Customers have seldom been
asked to do so. Similarly, investments in nontraditional distribution channels, such as supermarket minibranches, home and telephone banking,
and specialist jumbo mortgage networks, have failed to reduce the number of bank branches, which increased from 37,016 in 1980 to 56,512 in
1995. In addition, downstreaming of data entry for auto loans by giving
terminals to auto dealers has also often not led to a reduction in loan
processing workforces (or cost reductions have been offset by price
breaks for the dealers) and so on.

This is not to say that most investment programs have not made sense,
nor that any of the investments discussed here have been ineffective for
particular banks that have managed out the projected cost savings and

Figure 2.8

U.S. Commercial Banks—Headcount and Systems
Spending, 1960–1990 (Estimated)

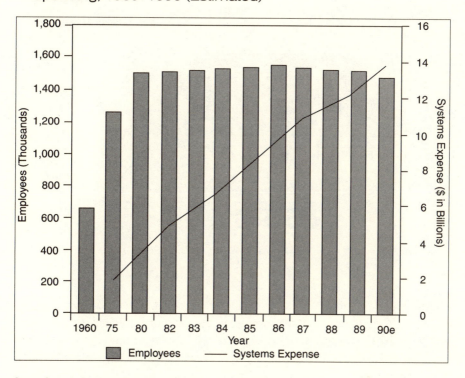

Source: Center for Information Technology and Strategy, Ernst & Young.

educated customers on how to use the new offerings. Citicorp, for example, is said to have achieved an 80 percent penetration rate for frequent usage of its ATMs. In general, however, the industry has often merely added another block of cost to the edifice of the past.

The Resulting Organizational Monstrosity

Senior and middle bank managers face an enormous cost challenge. The banking business involves an inherently complex structure of process, function, physical plant, and systems costs to service multiple customers,

Figure 2.9

Orgnizational Hierarchy and Reengineering

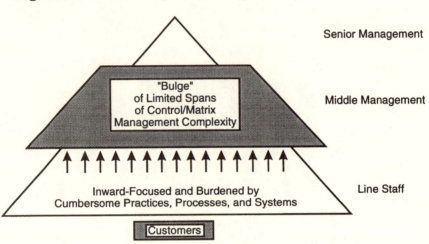

products, and geographies—even in a perfect world. The regulatory cocoon of the past created processes, practices, tasks, and traditions that further complicated the situation. The expenses of new geographic and product markets, as well as new forms of investment, were then overlaid on this dense muddled canvas.

Bankers have truly faced a "spaghetti cost" picture with the interwoven strands of cost complexity shown in Figure 2.2. The result is the organizational model depicted in Figure 2.9. Within this model, senior and middle management have grown into complex lines of business, geographic, and functional matrices (whether formally acknowledged in organization charts or not). As a result, middle management has bulged, with most executives having only three or four direct reports in order to maximize control. Most of their time is spent trying to manage complex relationships with their peers, satisfying multiple formal and informal bosses, and keeping ahead of potential crises below by imposing intricate control burdens down the line. As a result, the line staff has become inwardly-focused, spending inordinate amounts of time manipulating the same data for the trickle-down demands of innumerable control processes. This structure itself has bred costs.

THE MYSTERIES OF BANK COST ACCOUNTING

Given all these considerations, it would be helpful if the accounting methodologies used by bankers made sense. They often do not.

Once the regulatory and competitive cocoon of the past was broken, bankers scurried to try to disaggregate and understand their costs. Elaborate cost accounting systems were constructed, using traditional manufacturing cost accounting as their model. Detailed time and utilization studies were carried out to identify which resources were spent on each transaction; product; and, through transaction volumes, customer segment and geographic location. Process, function, plant, systems, and overhead costs were allocated by a range of indirect proxies—for example: headcount; square footage; asset or deposit levels pro rata to direct costs; and even, in some instances, the basic ability to pay. ("You earn more, so you can afford to pay more.") All the data were fed into a black box system that spewed forth reams of paper purporting to provide full-cost profitability for each product, each customer group, and each branch. And no one believed the results. Why?

Manufacturing Cost Accounting Inapplicable

First, the basic conceptual foundations of traditional cost accounting do not apply to highly common cost structures. Because most infrastructure expenses serve multiple customers, products, and geographies, any attempt to define them as attributable to a particular segment, transaction, or location is futile. Exit a customer market, a product, or a branch and many costs will not go away—they will simply have to be reallocated to what remains. The number of times strategic decisions have been made based on the fiction of full-cost allocations is saddening. In one instance, a major U.S. money center bank closed 20 branches only to have to reopen new locations (at subscale) once the true cost and revenue dynamics of the channels were understood. It sacrificed 3 percent of market share, saved almost no cost, and almost destroyed its franchise in the process by signaling that it had no commitment to the market.

System Obsolete Before It Starts

The banking industry has become so dynamic that the information contained in the elaborate accounting systems was out of date before the first printout was distributed. Moreover, keeping the system up to date was impossible. Resource commitments were simply too fluid in the banks' common cost environment to track. There was no steady-state production line to use as a norm.

The Best Negotiator Wins

Because no one believed the numbers as they were produced, the accounting systems inevitably became the basis for horse trading: if you did not like the results produced, you challenged the arcane methodologies that gave rise to them. Shout loudest and your numbers would be adjusted to keep you quiet—costs would be reallocated to a meeker executive.

One senior manager in a major New York bank, for example, has based his stellar career simply on renegotiating in each of his successive positions the allocations accepted by his predecessor. Since the mid-1980s, it has been amazing to note the credibility given to his successive "turn-arounds" of businesses—that were in fact achieved by smoke and mirrors.

Given the myriad challenges that bankers have to deal with, the last thing they needed was to have to face them with one hand tied behind their backs because of inappropriate, meaningless measurement systems. Yet, many significant capital investments, strategic divestments, and market entrances and exits were based on such deceptive numbers.

THE RESPONSE TO EXISTING COST STRUCTURES

Section Two of this report will address in detail how to face the challenge of disentangling the complexity of bank costs. Briefly, the core steps are as follows:

Redesign Processes, Not Tasks

In line with the Hammer and Champy philosophy, the crux of bank reengineering is not to optimize the efficiency of particular tasks—for example, time-and-motion benchmarks for tellerproof or credit checks—but rather the process flow from each input to its cumulative output. It is about doing better things, not about doing the same things in a better way at lower cost. Reengineering has to be done in a comprehensive, bankwide context, however, because of the interdependencies among and between the bank's infrastructure and management cost levers. This involves doing away with the baggage of past accounting methodologies and attacking costs where they fall, not allocating them through meaningless formulae.

Combine "Top-Down" and "Bottom-Up" Thinking

Reengineering cannot be simply a set of mandates from senior management, or theoretical redesign by outsiders. Neither can it be driven solely by troops in the trenches fixing the processes that create the task burdens that fall on them. The directions for radical new approaches to banking have to come from above. And the translation of these into the web of interlocking process implications down the line has to involve all staff members.

Energize the Bank for Change

Reengineering banks is about the management of change and being a catalyst for cultural change as much as it is about process, system, and structural redesign. This requires senior management to show a commitment to:

- ✦ Change—in terms of its time and the organization's resources.
- ✦ Fairness—in terms of openness to all ideas for change and of equitable treatment for affected staff.
- ✦ Involvement—in terms of total staff empowerment and open and frank communications.

Structure a Disciplined, Finite Approach

If reengineering a single process is itself challenging, both intellectually and in its need for energy for change, reengineering the entire bank can potentially be a nightmare. No organization can face an indefinite period of change without creating institutional chaos. With a highly structured approach over an inviolable intense time frame, however, not only can the challenge be met, but also a better, more focused, sales-oriented culture can be created, with more loyal and more confident staff members who are motivated to be winners. Chapters 5–12 will show how this can be achieved.

CHAPTER 3

The Pricing Impact
of the Past

INTRODUCTION

Although banks have so far failed to understand the true nature of their complex common cost structures and reengineer them, they have also woefully underpriced for: transaction services to reflect the true value they provide; geographic differences in relative price sensitivity; and the specific risk of commercial borrowers.

Moreover, banks attempting to adjust the inadequate pricing of the past must battle consumer advocate groups and antitrust regulators, which will make repricing in the future even more difficult.

In this chapter the reasons for this underpricing and its impact will be summarized, the risks of increased legislative and regulatory pricing controls considered, and practical steps for rectifying past mispricing outlined.

THE RESULTS OF PAST ERRORS

Banks have systematically underpriced for transaction services, geographic price differentials, and commercial loans, on a risk-adjusted basis.

Transaction Services Undervalued

A senior consumer banker has said of transaction pricing: "We base our prices on judgment. If the product sells, we were right. If it doesn't sell, we lower the price." Another banker recalled how her bank set the price for a highly successful new product: "We thought $1.50 was too high, and $1.30 seemed like an odd number, so we settled on $1.25." This is not the way to price. Across all product lines within the banking industry, the results of such lack of pricing sophistication are evident:

- One U.S. bank's trust department charged its customers a standard annual charge, although 80 percent of low-balance customers accounted for 90 percent of costs but only 10 percent of revenues.

- Another's retail credit department charged merchants $533 per annum for card services, compared with its annual direct cost of $574, and charged its customers $30 per card annually, whereas each cost $44.

- In another example, no charge was imposed for expensive on-site collateral inspections for asset-based loans.

Why have bankers failed to price effectively for commercial cash management information services, consumer deposit return items, small business rolls of change, custody accounts, and so on? In the old days, bankers had little need to develop expertise in setting prices for specific transactions. Regulation Q provided a price umbrella for retail deposits that made it unnecessary to understand the specific value that customers placed on individual services and transactions. Products were bundled for pricing purposes, cross-subsidies between services flourished, and understanding costs and margins was of little importance.

In 1980, when the winds of deregulation shredded the price umbrella, institutions were forced to set their own prices. Cost-based pricing and competition-based pricing became popular. Yet both were inward-looking approaches by the industry, rather than outward-focused approaches to customers' needs and behavior. Both resulted in mispricing.

Cost-Based Pricing

The formula used in cost-based pricing is cost plus margin, which obviously means that the bank must know what its costs are. It has been shown that most banks had no true understanding of their costs at the time of deregulation, and that although many embarked on the painstaking task of allocating costs to products or customers, they used the standard unit costing methodologies of manufacturing companies (which are essentially meaningless in banks) to allocate common costs.

Pricing off such fictitious costs led to absurd decisions. For example, a fad in the late 1980s (that is reemerging today) was for consultants to dredge the bank's customer information files and provide a fully-costed profitability analysis of all consumer demand deposit accounts (including allocations for the corporate jet). Not surprisingly, an "80/90/20" rule was observed: 80 percent of the customers accounted for 90 percent of costs and 20 percent of revenues. Moreover, the bottom 10 percent of customers accounted for 40 percent of costs and 5 percent of revenues. Did this present a repricing opportunity? Perhaps. The response was, however, to argue that the 80 percent should be repriced to "bring them up" to the level of profitability of the 20 percent. Not only did this ignore that the allocated 90 percent of costs was a fiction, but it also led to dramatic account runoffs (with resulting reallocation of costs), significant Community Reinvestment Act problems, and overall decimation of returns on consumer liability products.

The furor over Citibank's attempts in the mid-1980s to force low-balance customers to use ATMs by effectively banning them from teller lines (an experiment that lasted only a few hours) and First Chicago's explicit charges for teller access in 1995 are good examples of cost accounting overcoming common sense. Fictional costs beget aberrant pricing. A more significant argument against cost-based pricing, however, is that it ignores customer price elasticity, that is, the ratio of the percent change in demand caused by a percent change in price.

Customer market research provides compelling evidence that customers value bank services far more than bankers think they do. In an *American Banker* survey, consumers ranked price as the seventh most important factor in dealing with a bank. Such price insensitivity is reflected in the incredible loyalty that customers have for their banks. Almost 50 percent of businesses with sales under $5 million have been with their primary banks for 10 years or more. For individual consumers, that number jumps to more than 60 percent. Moreover, 76 percent of small business customers were either "very satisfied" or "satisfied" with their bank. Only 6 percent were "dissatisfied." Similarly, for consumers, 66 percent of customers were very satisfied with their banks. Research has also consistently shown that most customers say that the quality of service at their primary bank is better than, or as good as, that of service-conscious businesses such as hotels and restaurants.[1]

But the true test is in actually raising prices. If a bank raises its prices beyond the value that customers attach to its products, they will simply vote with their feet by taking their business elsewhere. My experience has shown that prices can be selectively raised, provided products and services are

---

1   *American Banker*, Special Marketing section, September 1994.

unbundled and carefully reviewed, based on perceived customer value instead of cost-plus pricing.

This is not restricted to markets where competition is scarce. Even when customers have the option to switch institutions, banks can increase their transaction revenues by 15 to 20 percent simply by adopting selective repricing based on customer value—with less than 1 percent account runoff, and even that concentrated in very low balance accounts. This is not to suggest that a thorough knowledge of costs—at least direct costs—has no place in the price-setting process. In fact, it enables institutions to see what price levels are unsustainable in view of existing capacity and competitor prices. Although knowledge of costs is a necessary element in effective pricing, it is not sufficient to price optimally.

Competition-Based Pricing

Knowledge of competitors' prices is valuable in the same way. Often, however, financial institutions rely on the market or major competitors to set the correct price levels. Competition-based pricing has two major drawbacks:

- A price follower frequently adopts the leader's price without giving much thought as to whether the company's cost structure can support that price.
- Customer price elasticity is often not considered.

At times, competition-based prices can be advantageous if a price leader is maintaining a price umbrella at levels that give most institutions comfortable margins and if high entry barriers are preventing invasion by new entrants. Such a price umbrella helps an institution put things in perspective while answering the following questions:

- Are our prices in line with those of our competitors?
- Can we make a profit at prevailing prices?
- Are the market prices an indication of the industry's cost structure?
- If so, are we a low-cost or a high-cost producer?

Yet price leaders often do not know any better than followers what constitutes the right price when balanced against perceived value.

Value-Based Pricing

The limitations of existing pricing practices should be contrasted with value-based pricing, which is rooted in customer behavior, and—only

FIGURE 3.1

Philadelphia Bank Example—Business Premium Savings

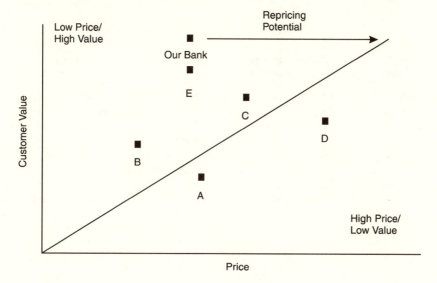

then—factors in cost and competition. Such an approach focuses explicitly on customer price elasticity at the transactional level.

Figure 3.1 illustrates the concept of perceived value versus competitors' prices and shows an example of a Philadelphia bank's pricing for business savings accounts. The bank had been charging a price discount for a service value premium. Adjusting prices led to a 15 percent increase in transaction revenues. Relative sensitivity to price is a function of many financial and psychological factors, most typically amount of payment; frequency of purchase; complexity of product; pricing structure; switching cost; availability of information; and image, as shown in Table 3.1.

Although not all of these factors come into play in every case, some examples will demonstrate their importance.

Amount of Payment   Not surprisingly, price elasticity is higher for bigger-ticket items. Credit card and mortgage interest rates are a clear example. Whereas 88 percent of cardholders felt that banks were "taking advantage" of customers through the credit card rates that they charged, only 1 percent switched banks following significant price challenges by competitors. The monthly cash flow associated with card balances is so low

TABLE 3.1

Factors Affecting Price Sensitivity

Type of Lever	Factors Affecting Price Elasticity	Price Elasticity*	
		Low	High
Attribute	Amount of payment	Small	Large
Attribute	Frequency of payment	Low	High
Attribute	Complexity of product	Complex Bundled	Simple Single
Attribute	Pricing structure	Obscure with hidden charges	Simple and explicit
Attribute	Switching cost	High	Low
Perception	Availability of information	Unavailable Hard to comprehend	Readily available Easy to comprehend
Perception	Image	Sophisticated "High class"	Plain "Workhorse"

* Low price elasticity means that customers are indifferent to price levels; price elasticity is high when customers react strongly to a small change in price.

for most customers that it is insignificant when compared with the inconvenience of switching accounts (particularly given the perception of the annual fee as a sunk cost). In contrast the 1992–1993 and 1996 mortgage refinancing binges in the United States reflects mortgage customers' intense sensitivity to the much higher monthly payments for home financing.

Complexity of Product   The opportunity cost of understanding transaction fees for such bundled products as cash management accounts makes many customers simply ignore the charges for the product. One bank's survey found that 20 percent of customers did not even open and read their statements, let alone reconcile the account fees. Similarly, for credit cards, research has shown that awareness of the charges for late payment, foreign exchange purchases, and teller/ATM withdrawals were respectively 5 percent, 0 percent, and 3 percent. Yet, such charges provide almost 10 percent of most banks' total revenue from cards. Nonetheless, a 20-basis-point difference in certificate of deposit (CD) rates can result in the flight of significant amounts of "hot money."

Image   Gold credit cards are an obvious example of image value. The value of the card is perceived to be high, even though the incremental costs of added services are minimal—and the majority of such services often do not, in fact, add to customer perceived value. In one instance a 20 percent higher annual fee was charged for services that cost only 5 percent more to provide, and usage rates for most of the add-on services were negligible. By contrast, removal of a frequent flyer affiliation in a second situation led to a 30 percent reduction in charge volume. In subsequent chapters a practical approach on how value-based pricing can lead to increases of 15–20 percent of total bank noninterest income with minimal (if any) account runoff will be outlined. This, applied across the whole of the U.S. banking system, could lead to incremental pretax earnings of $12 billion to $15 billion.[2]

Geographic Pricing Undifferentiated

Federal Reserve Board studies found that: "As mergers cause banking power to be concentrated in fewer hands, particularly in states like California, where the market is already more concentrated than elsewhere, depositors tend to earn lower interest rates. And borrowers, particularly small businesses, are charged higher rates for loans." Is this surprising?

As Figure 3.2 illustrates, on August 13, 1991, personal loans in Los Angeles were priced at 20.3 percent, while NOW checking accounts were paying 4.0 percent. In Philadelphia on the same day personal loans were priced at 14.6 percent, whereas NOW accounts paid almost 4.6 percent. It has been argued that this reflects the fact that California's largest banks hold 20 to 30 percent shares in their local county markets.[3]

Analysis by Timothy Hannan of the Federal Reserve[4] has shown that borrowers in markets with a concentrated banking system pay interest rates 50 to 220 basis points above what borrowers pay in the least concentrated markets, depending on the type of loan.[5]

---

2   Analysis for 1995, based on information supplied by Ferguson & Company, March 1997.

3   Michael Quint, "Giant Banks: Will the Little Guy Pay?" *New York Times*, August 23, 1991.

4   Timothy Hannan, "Foundations of the Structure-Conduct-Performance Paradigm," *Finance and Economic Discussion Series, No 83*, Board of Governors of the Federal Reserve System, 1989.

5   Michael Keely and Gary Zimmerman, "Determining Geographic Markets for Deposit Competition in Banking," *Economic Review,* Federal Reserve Bank of San Francisco, pp. 25–45, 1985.

FIGURE 3.2

Geographic Pricing Differentiation—Average Interest Rates

Personal Loans		NOW Checking
Los Angeles	20.25%	4.03%
San Francisco	19.12%	4.06%
New York	18.35%	4.45%
Boston	17.69%	4.85%
Average Bank	17.37%	4.49%
Chicago	16.85%	4.58%
Washington	16.78%	5.03%
Dallas	16.61%	4.76%
Avg. savings and loan	16.54%	4.65%
Houston	16.11%	4.78%
Detroit	15.00%	4.60%
Philadelphia	14.64%	4.57%

Source: *New York Times.*

Is there justifiable cause for concern that, with consolidation, "the little guy will pay," thereby supporting consumer advocate concerns? The differentials in deposit and lending yields are most often a reflection of the removal of irrational local pricing rather than the gouging of consumer and small business customers. In nearly every market that I have examined, a higher share of distribution coverage gives rise to a disproportionate share of customer penetration, irrespective of price. Figure 3.3 illustrates, for two random markets, the relationship between the number of retail outlets an institution has and the amount of its market share. In each case, the lead bank was not paying for market share.

This phenomenon is the result of the fact that, from the customers' perspective, competitors are rewarded for having a higher share of

FIGURE 3.3

Branch Density Impact in Selected Local Markets

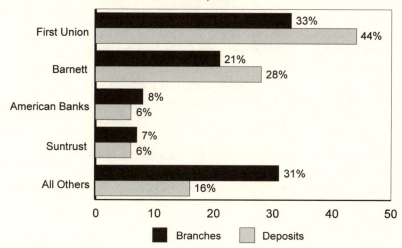

Jacksonville, Florida
100% = 214 branches
100% = $7.2 billion deposits

- First Union — Branches 33%, Deposits 44%
- Barnett — Branches 21%, Deposits 28%
- American Banks — Branches 8%, Deposits 6%
- Suntrust — Branches 7%, Deposits 6%
- All Others — Branches 31%, Deposits 16%

■ Branches   ▢ Deposits

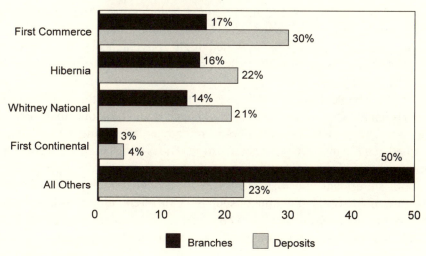

New Orleans, Louisiana
100% = 258 branches
100% = $10.6 billion deposits

- First Commerce — Branches 17%, Deposits 30%
- Hibernia — Branches 16%, Deposits 22%
- Whitney National — Branches 14%, Deposits 21%
- First Continental — Branches 3%, Deposits 4%
- All Others — Branches 50%, Deposits 23%

■ Branches   ▢ Deposits

Source: Ferguson & Company.

distribution locations and the right type of distribution (such as branch or ATM distribution) in the right place. In a bank survey, 80 percent of customers said they chose their main bank on the basis of convenience to home, and over 60 percent defined convenience as involving less than five minutes' travel. This is not surprising, given that nearly 50 percent of the customers said they visited their branch at least once a week, and is no different from McDonalds restaurants or other consumer chains which have understood that they can achieve a price premium for providing convenient distribution networks. In short, as for all retailers, the three key factors for bank distribution value are "location, location, location." The nature of what constitutes "location" is undergoing radical change, and the changes will accelerate. However, perceived "convenience," no matter how defined, will remain a critical customer preference.

Are customers therefore irrational? I believe consumers and small business entrepreneurs are highly rational in their criteria for selecting suppliers. Reason, however, does not always equal price. Customers value the perceived advantage of convenience well ahead of price. As a result certain community banking strategies, even by large-scale regional banks, pay dividends. KeyCorp of Albany, New York, for example, prior to its merger with Society Bank, provided and charged for the value of local community convenience with significant success.[6] It had acquired 11 banks by the mid-1990s and achieved an average ROE of 16 percent versus the industry average of 12 percent. Its strategy was to acquire small rural banks with a dominant local share and to concentrate on providing, and pricing explicitly for, excellent service. KeyCorp's management understood that local concentrated markets provided high convenience (and perceived commitment to the community) where it could give value to customers that they would pay for.

Many banks have failed, however, to capitalize on this potential for local pricing differentials. Later in this chapter it will be shown that bankers face significant regulatory barriers to remedying the results of past fragmented, regulated, local price competition. The pricing potential of concentration— provided it does not overstep the bounds of antitrust constraints— is both significant and justified by customer behavioral preferences. A rough estimate of the potential of such price differentiation is as high as $6 billion pretax annually for the whole of the U.S. banking industry. Yet, regulators and consumer groups will not readily accept repricing.

---

6   Key Corporation Annual Reports, 1988–1992.

Commercial Loan Pricing Inadequate

Banks have also failed to price effectively for their true cost of lending, once the relative risk of borrowers is taken into account. This is especially true of the commercial lending arena because of the effect of the changes in both demand and supply factors during the 1980s (see Chapter 1) that dramatically changed commercial loan pricing.

As Harrison Young, the FDIC's former director of resolutions, has said, "I don't think the commercial lending business works anymore. . . . Banks aren't getting paid for equity risk."[7]

To recap the pricing issue briefly: commercial loan demand has decreased because capital market alternatives such as commercial paper, medium-term notes, junk bonds, and derivatives (such as swaps) have provided more efficient and less expensive options for all maturities for all but the riskiest borrowers. Meanwhile, alternative suppliers such as foreign banks, insurance companies, and finance companies have made significant inroads into the market.

The result is overcapacity without rationalization of competition. Weak lenders have not exited, nor has a new, lower-cost approach to bank lending been created (although the fledgling securitization market for commercial loans may help to rectify this). In part, this has been because bankers have not understood the marginal cost of lending on a risk-adjusted basis. Figure 3.4 shows the result of comparing the spread over LIBOR (the London Interbank Offering Rate) for the commercial loans of a 30-bank sample with their credit quality categories versus the implicit spreads in the bond market for comparable issues, ranked by their Standard and Poor's (S&P's) ratings.

Banks have simply been underpricing for the commercial loan risk—often essentially equity risk—that they have assumed. A very rough estimate of the annual impact on the U.S. banking industry of such underpricing may be as high as $4 billion pretax.

FORCES TO COUNTER REPRICING

Banks have systematically underpriced for the value of nonbalance transaction services, geographic differentiation relative to local distribution convenience, and commercial loans on a risk-adjusted basis. A gross estimate of the cumulative pretax profit potential of these past errors is $25

---

7   *American Banker*, October 1, 1993

FIGURE 3.4

Corporate Risk-Reward Price

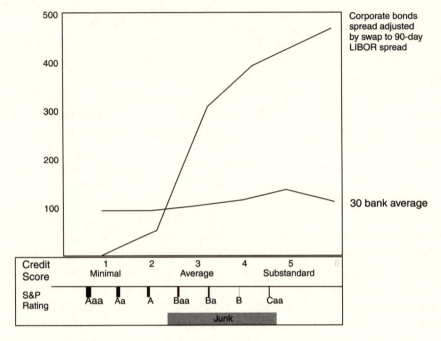

Yield over LIBOR (In Basis Points)

Source: *American Banker.*

billion annually (20 percent of 1996 bank earnings). Will these lost earnings be realized? Significant forces are developing to counter rational market repricing both from regulators and from consumer activists.

Regulatory Intervention

Five U.S. regulatory challenges illustrate the very real threat to rational pricing.

First Hawaiian

When First Hawaiian sought to acquire First Interstate of Hawaii, the Justice Department sought to impose a test of market concentration based on the market for loans to small and medium-sized businesses, instead of employing the traditional Herfindahl-Hirschman Index (HHI) test of local deposit share. First Hawaiian believed the department, using its test, overestimated its small business market share by 1,000 percent. Yet even the traditional HHI test is overly restrictive, as it undervalues:

- Nonbank suppliers of services (even with the 50 percent thrift deposit exception).

- The potential for structural change in a market which is a prime target for new entrants but is already concentrated because of past regulatory barriers.

- Overall competitor positions, paralyzing a small bank with high market share in only one or two counties, while potentially benefiting larger institutions with fragmented low deposit shares in many markets—which are often subscale as retailers.

The Justice Department's intervention in the First Hawaiian transaction caused a five-month delay in closing, yet led to the divestment of only six branches and one finance company office.

Fleet/Bank of New England
The Justice Department's intervention in Fleet's acquisition of the defunct Bank of New England's distribution network, because of concerns regarding overconcentration, forced the divestment of only six branches having $87 million of deposits in three markets in Maine.

Norwest/First Federal
In 1991 the Federal Reserve rejected Minneapolis-based Norwest Corporation's application to acquire First Federal of Rapid City, South Dakota, on the grounds that the deal would create anticompetitive results. As a result, no acquisition materialized and more than half of First Federal's branches were closed.

Texas Commerce Bancshares/First City Bank
The Federal Reserve rejected Texas Commerce's bid for First City because the Chemical Banking Corporation affiliate was already the number one lender to middle-market companies and small businesses in the affected areas.

Firstar/Waterloo Savings
The Iowa division of Milwaukee-based Firstar withdrew its application in May 1993 to acquire Waterloo Savings Bank after the Justice Department found the Waterloo market to be highly concentrated and indicated that

significant divestitures would be required to win approval. The considerable delays and expense of the process led the companies to terminate their merger agreement.

Misconceived Approach to Competition

The above examples illustrate a misconceived approach to competition in the U.S. market deriving from:

- The ability at the time of acquisition for the Federal Reserve and the Justice Department to impose a new standard of competitive concentration and control.
- The easy-target nature of banks for regulatory intervention since the 1930s.
- The absence of convincing and empirically-based lobbying efforts by banks to illustrate that pricing reflects past aberrations.

Consumer Activist Group Misinterpretations

A survey report released by the U.S. Public Interest Research Group and the Consumer Federation of America, which accuses banks of charging "exorbitant" fees to customers, further exemplifies the significant forces developing to counter rational pricing. The group accused banks of ". . . having a three-tier strategy to cheat consumers: higher fees; higher minimum balance requirements; and new types of fees."[8]

When countered by the argument that bank costs were rising, the group replied that extensive documentation showed that bank costs had actually been declining. It failed to take into account, however, the underlying reasons for reductions in bank costs. Credit costs, for example, have declined because banks have at last begun to restore the balance sheet strength lost because of deteriorating asset values in the late 1980s. Higher loan rates reflect the true level of commercial loan risk and protect the industry from repeating the mistakes of the past.

Deposit prices have similarly declined in the United States because commercial banks no longer have to compete with weak, government-propped savings and loan associations offering irrationally high deposit

---

8   *American Banker*, June 6, 1993.

rates. The elimination of these institutions, coupled with low interest rates, has allowed banks to reprice deposits. The difficulty in countering most consumer advocate analyses of bank pricing is that they take an arbitrary historical starting point and make comparisons based thereon. Because past pricing levels were wrong on a value- and risk-adjusted basis, the whole comparison is flawed.

THE RESPONSE TO MISPRICING

Later chapters will discuss in detail the specific steps to counter the results of past errors in pricing, and to realize the benefits of value-based transaction pricing; geographically differentiated pricing; and risk-based lending. In brief, however, a number of steps are required.

Price to Value

Transactions and services have a definable and quantifiable value to customers. Bankers must step back from the apparent reassurance of cost-based pricing, or "that's what competitor X charges, so will we," and follow consumer product marketing standards of value pricing.

Price Geographically

Bankers have to understand that customers will pay differentiated prices for the local distribution convenience they provide. Customers are not irrational in failing to arbitrage geographic price differences—they understand the forgone income or cost but trade it off against what they value more highly: local convenience.

Price Loans for Differential Risk

Bankers must break down the respective risk of different borrower segments (in the same way that investment bankers do with mortgage-backed securities or insurance companies do with pockets of car insurance risk) to differentiate their loan pricing.

Lobby for Rational Pricing

Just as bankers are becoming aware of their irrational pricing of the past, regulators and consumer advocates are using earlier mistakes as the empirical basis for denying future rationality. A significant educational process is required to illustrate the justification for future repricing to allow price and value to be brought back into equilibrium.

ADDITIONAL SOURCES

Austin, Douglas, "The Herfindahl-Hirschman Index: Analysing its Effectiveness," *Issues in Bank Regulation*, Summer 1988.

Berger, Allen and Timothy Hanna, "The Price-Concentration Relationship in Banking," *Review of Economics and Statistics 71*, 1989.

Ballenbacher, George and Joseph Walton, "Shakeout Won't Shrink Industry to a Few Mammoth Banks," *American Banker,* March 9, 1994.

Demsetz, Harold, "Industry Structure, Market Rivalry, and Public Policy," *Journal of Law and Economics 16,* 1973.

Flannery, Mark, "Retail Bank Deposits as Quasi-Fixed Factors of Production," *American Economic Review 72*, 1982.

Gilbert, Alton, "Studies of Bank Market Structure and Competition: A Review and Evaluation," *Journal of Money, Credit, and Banking 16*, 1984.

Neuberger, Jonathan, and Gary Zimmerman, "The California Deposit Rate Mystery," *Weekly Letter*, Federal Reserve Bank of San Francisco, January 27, 1989.

Peltzman, Samuel, "The Gains and Losses from Industrial Concentration," *Journal of Law and Economics 20*, 1977.

Smirlock, Michael, "Evidence of the (Non) Relationship between Concentration and Profitability in Banking," *Journal of Money, Credit and Banking*, 1985.

CHAPTER 4

When to Reengineer

INTRODUCTION

The first three chapters of this book have shown why reengineering is critical to future competitive success: the banking industry's costs are too high and its prices too low. This chapter will outline when a bank's board of directors and CEO should step up to the reengineering challenge. Two distinct situations should be considered: the stand-alone bank and, following merger or acquisition, the consolidating bank.

THE STAND-ALONE BANK

Bank chairpersons often bemoan their bank's languishing stock prices, arguing that the market is undervaluing the strength of their underlying customer and business franchises. U.S. bank stocks sold in October 1996 at a discount of 26 percent to the Standard & Poor's 500 stock index at an average price/earnings multiple of 12.6 times versus the overall market multiple of 17.1 times.[1] The way in which the market values bank stocks and its implications for the reengineering decision will be reviewed.

---

1   SNL Securities, Charlottesville, VA; Barron's, October 1996.

FIGURE 4.1

Divergent Performance Reflected in Price Multiples
Midwest Banks

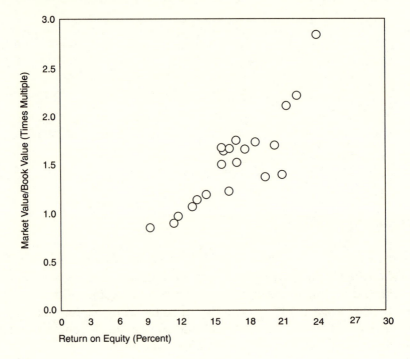

Source: SNL Securities.

Market Valuation

Empirical evidence shows that there is a direct correlation between ROE and stock market trading multiples to book value, as demonstrated in Figure 4.1.

Another crucial measure of performance which underlies ROE is the efficiency ratio (which divides noninterest expense minus foreclosed property expense by the sum of net interest income, on a fully taxable equivalent basis, and noninterest income). This ratio is increasingly viewed as a superior indicator of relative performance because more traditional meas-

FIGURE 4.2

Correlation between Efficiency and P/E Ratios for Sample Commercial Banks

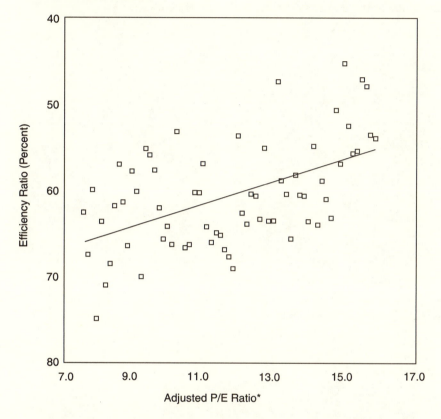

*Adjusted to exclude extraordinary items, securities gains and losses, and nonrecurring items.

Source: *The SNL Quarterly Bank Digest.*

ures, such as expenses to assets, have been affected by securitization, private placements, derivatives, and other forms of off-balance sheet financing. The linkage of shareholder value to the efficiency ratio (cents of cost required to generate each dollar of revenue) is clear, as shown in Figure 4.2.

U.S. banks are not efficient. Figure 4.3 shows the distribution in performance for the industry. The average efficiency ratio between 1987

FIGURE 4.3

Commercial Bank Efficiency Ratios

U.S. Publicly Traded Banks (Asset Size > $1.5 Billion)

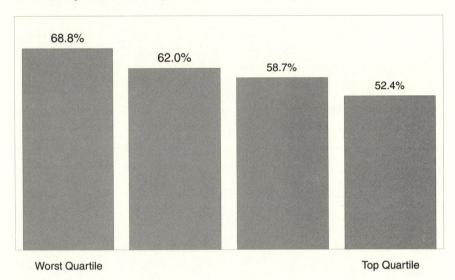

Worst Quartile   Top Quartile

All U.S. Publicly Traded Banks

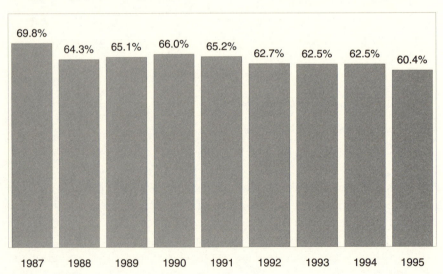

Source: SNL Securities.

and 1995 was about 64 percent, despite all the talk of consolidation and restructuring efficiencies. Although the ratio appears to improve in 1992–1995, this is primarily the result of high levels of loan growth, net interest margin and trading revenues, and, if the ratio's denominator is adjusted for these supernormal revenues, productivity in fact would have remained basically flat.

Nonetheless, the top-quartile bank performers have an efficiency ratio of 52 percent. For a $5 billion bank (with an average business mix), the differential between the average and the top performer efficiency ratios can amount to about $30 million in incremental net income and 60 basis points of return on assets, explaining the stock market's premium for banks with superior efficiency ratios.[2]

For a stand-alone bank's board of directors and CEO the inevitable question becomes, "Where is the source of improvement for such productivity advantage?" Assessing the levers for bank return improvement suggests that operating performance enhancement—the basic reengineering of process cost and price—is a major source of sustained earnings gains.

Leverage

Additional financial management of returns is not viable for most banks, given the basic nature of their balance sheets and regulatory controls of capital adequacy. Indeed, compliance with the Bank for International Settlements' capital requirements and risk-based capital standards since 1989 has forced the industry to deleverage.

Tax Advantages

Any gains from a tax management perspective in the U.S. context were largely removed by the Tax Reform Act of 1986.

Short-Term Business Portfolio Breakup

The high level of common costs shared by different customer segments for multiple products across dispersed geographic locations means that spinning off businesses to shareholders or acquirers is extremely difficult for banks. There are exceptions such as the sale of mortgage servicing rights, the sale by MNC Financial of MBNA Corporation, and the sale of Capital

---

2   ABDR, SNL Securities.

One by Signet Corporation to the public. The economics of the core businesses of banking, however, simply do not currently facilitate this form of disaggregation for short-term shareholder value creation.

Strategic Advantage

Chapters 1 to 3 described the revenue crunch that banks faced from the decline in one-time securities gains and supernormal interest margin profits, their developing obsolescence in commercial lending, fierce competition for retail assets and liabilities, and the rise of nonbank players. Many of the traditionally most attractive banking markets have excess capacity supplied by banks and new entrants. As a result, any sustained growth has to be the result of either market share gains at the expense of others, or by acquisition. The rise of cherry picking by nonbanks of such products as credit cards are, however, going to make "growing into" the required cost/revenue relationship exceptionally difficult. Yet, many bankers are still waiting for market share growth to save the day.

A bank's board of directors and CEO have to take a long, hard look at management's "hockey stick" strategic plan projections, and challenge the underlying rationale for business turnarounds and share penetration.

I am not a dire pessimist about banking's future, given the industry's real competitive advantages, such as its branch networks, payment and transaction processing capabilities, superior credit underwriting skills, and customer franchise value. This is true, however, only if banks adjust their fundamental operating performance to create a viable economic basis for competition.

The Reengineering Decision

When should the CEO know that the core bank requires reengineering? The following are five telltale signs.

Languishing Stock Price

The market is telegraphing bankers that it is focusing on long-term earnings growth potential as the basis for its valuation of their stocks. The trend toward discount in multiples reflects a shareholder view that the industry is being complacent in response to the market's concerns. Contrast State Street Boston Corporation and Fifth Third Bancorp with the industry as a whole. Both have significant transaction-processing businesses that provide annuity streams of fee-based earnings. They sell respectively at a market/book multiple of 2.8 times and 3.0 times, and both sell at a price/earnings multiple of 17 times. The industry as a whole has multiples of 1.6 times and 13.5 times.[3] A low market valuation of current earnings is a clear signal for dramatic action. The impact of reengineering can be illustrated by the performance of the stock of Star Banc, First Security Corporation, and CoreStates Financial Corporation following the announcement of their reengineering efforts (Figure 4.4).

Strategic Directions Conflict with Market Valuation

To the extent that the board and the CEO are committed to remaining independent and growing, either internally or through acquisitions, the market's signals test the viability of their strategy. Low multiples will both attract potential predators and limit acquisitions because of the dilution of ever more vocal institutional investors that result from bank purchases with undervalued paper.

Conversely, to the extent that the strategy is to "dress the bank up for sale," the distribution of acquisition premiums versus performance shown in Figure 4.5 clearly demonstrates the value to shareholders of fixing the bank prior to its sale.

Sub-Par Efficiency Ratios

Comparisons of ratios have their limitations because of differences in business mix and other factors. State Street Boston has an efficiency ratio of 74 percent, for example, reflecting the high fixed-cost structure of its processing businesses.[4] As a rule of thumb, however, the efficiency ratio is a leading indicator of competitive positioning. A small to medium-sized regional bank should have an efficiency ratio of 50 percent or less if it is to be a major force in the future. Significant divergence from this level is a sure sign of imbalance between the bank's revenue-generation potential and its cost base.

Perceived Process Redundancy

The signals above are hard, quantitative clues of the potential for reengineering. Even more important are the soft indicators of process misdesign.

---

3   SNL Securities.

4   Ibid.

FIGURE 4.4

Stock Market Rewards Reengineering–CoreStates Financial Corporation, First Security Corporation, and Star Banc Corporation

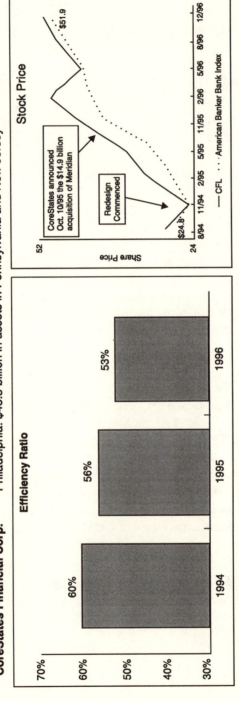

CoreStates Financial Corp.   Philadelphia: $45.5 billion in assets in Pennsylvania and New Jersey

Total Market Valuation increased $3.8 billion.

FIGURE 4.4

Continued

First Security Corporation   Salt Lake City: $14.7 billion in assets in Utah, Idaho, Wyoming, New Mexico, Oregon, Nevada

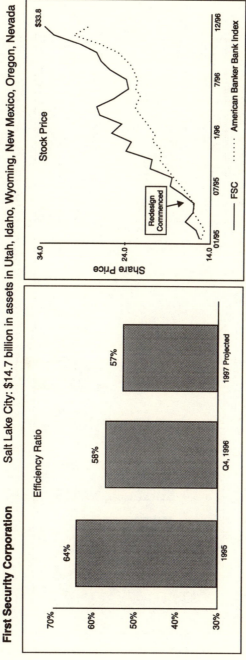

Total Market Valuation increased $1.5 billion. For the period 4/95–12/96 American Banker Bank Index rose 84% while First Security rose 118%.

FIGURE 4.4

Concluded

Star Banc Corporation Cincinnati: $10.1 billion in assets in Ohio, Indiana, Kentucky

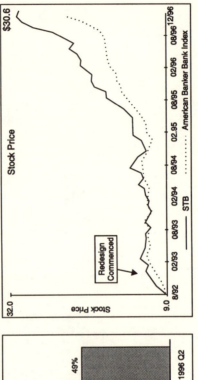

Total Market Valuation increased $1.9 billion 37% CGR. For the period 8/92–12/96 American Bank Index rose 145% while Star Banc rose 253%.

FIGURE 4.5

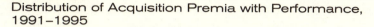

Distribution of Acquisition Premia with Performance, 1991–1995

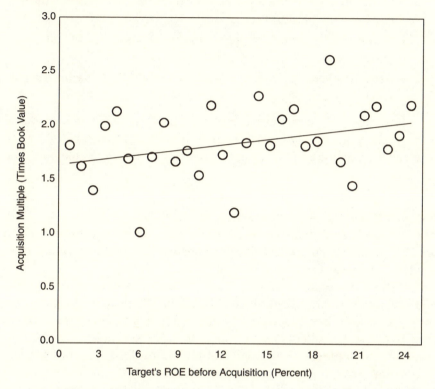

Source: *SNL Bank Mergers & Acquisitions.*

These may be identified by asking such questions as:

+ Are turnaround times for loan applications and suchlike slower than the market, and becoming more protracted in peak demand periods?
+ Are customer complaints on the rise?
+ Have significant expenditures on new technology and systems failed to produce demonstrable cost savings or revenue improvements?
+ Are senior managers spending much of their time dealing with administration and crisis management, rather than setting strategic direction and getting out to see customers?

- Do the paper-ridden desks of platform staff resemble rats' nests?
- How many staff members report to the average middle-level manager? How many layers of management exist between the CEO and the platform staff?
- Within the corporate culture, is success measured by the number of new sales or by the number of problems solved?
- Are employees aggressive and hungry for the bank's earnings success, or are they passive time servers?

It is astounding how much senior managements can learn in response to these questions simply by leaving their day-to-day concerns for a week or so, and asking the employees in the trenches what they do and how they feel about it.

Senior Management Will and Skill

The CEO and his team also have to ask themselves the hard question: "Do we have the stomach and capability to challenge everything we do from scratch?" An honest answer is critical.

Many bankers are justifiably proud of their heritage, their staff loyalty, and even their existing performance. Interestingly, reengineering is often most successful when undertaken by an already superior performer, where the CEO bites the bullet to take his institution to the next level of achievement and prepare it for the rough-and-tumble banking world of the late 1990s. Reengineering in true turnaround situations for weak banks is easier in one way—given the "do-or-die" environment—but can lead to management having a shorter-term perspective on customer service and risk.

For a good performer to face the intensity and uncertainty of reengineering takes vision and courage. Outsiders can facilitate the program and provide thought-leadership from past experience (the skills to help reengineer), but commitment and determination to succeed must come from within the bank.

THE CONSOLIDATING BANK

Following a merger or acquisition it might seem redundant to ask whether there is reengineering potential in the consolidating bank situation. Yet, given the industry's limited success to date in realizing the cost efficiencies and synergies that often were cited as the very justification for transactions, the issue is not moot. Will and skill for reengineering are as critical here as in the stand-alone bank. The industry's record to date and the appropriate approach to improving it will be considered.

Consolidation to Date

Over 3,200 private acquisitions of banks occurred between 1979 and 1995, amounting to $321 billion in purchase price (Figure 4.6). Moreover, the trend has progressively been toward larger target transactions, as acquirers have sought to achieve market scale and thereby greater potential savings and revenue benefits. As Table 4.1 shows, from 1989 to 1992 only 6 percent of all banks, but 20 percent of banks in the $5 billion–$10 billion asset size, had been acquired.

This search for scale is reflected in the premiums paid for acquisitions. Banks in the under $100 million asset range, for example, have sold for an average price/book multiple of 1.4 times and an average price/earnings ratio of 12.8 times, whereas those in the $1 billion–$5 billion range have sold for multiples of 1.8 times and 14.7 times, respectively.

Both stock market responses and academic research, however, raise doubts about the true cost/pricing potential of consolidation (at least for transactions that do not involve completely overlapping markets). As Table 4.2 demonstrates, the short-term stock market performance of acquirers involved in 22 large bank acquisitions since January 1991 has been less than stellar. Stock values declined on average 4 percent from the fifth day before the announcement of a transaction and the day after it was made (after adjusting for the overall movement in bank stocks during the same period). Figure 4.7 shows the longer-term stock performance of four in-market mega-deals that took place in 1991. Only Chemical has outpaced the overall bank sector's performance (a good sign for the Chase acquisition).

Academic research has supported the stock market's skepticism. Numerous studies have found that consolidations have only limited impact on cost. The Federal Reserve's Donald T. Savage found, for example, that even in-market transactions had minor benefits. In a hypothetical example involving the merger of a bank with $20 billion in assets and a bank with $10 billion in assets, where 100 branches were closed, Savage found that operating costs at the new bank actually rose 4.3 percent if there was no loss of customers. Even if the acquiring bank lost 20 percent of its assets and closed 100 branches, cost savings amounted to only 2.2 percent of the combined expenses of the two banks before their merger.[5]

---

5   Donald T. Savge, *Mergers, Branch Closures and Cost Savings,* Federal Reserve,
        May 1991.

FIGURE 4.6

Domestic Banking Mergers and Acquisitions

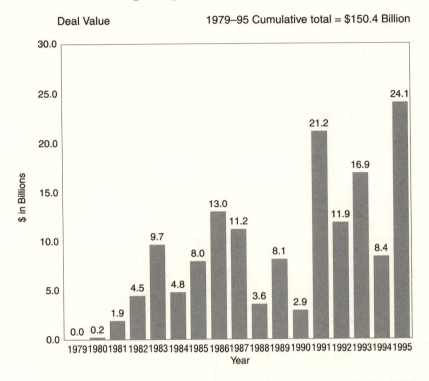

Deal Value   1979–95 Cumulative total = $150.4 Billion

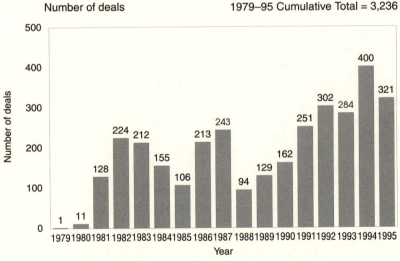

Number of deals   1979–95 Cumulative Total = 3,236

Sources: Securities Data Company; SNL Securities.

TABLE 4.1

Cumulative Bank Acquisitions by Asset Size, 1989–1992

Asset Size	Private Acquisitions since January 1989	As a Percentage of Banks in Category
Under $100 million	413	5.4
$100 million–500 million	147	7.1
$500 million–1 billion	17	7.6
$1 billion–5 billion	41	17.0
$5 billion–10 billion	11	20.4
Over $10 billion	7	10.3
Total	636	6.1

FIGURE 4.7

Market Performance of Four In-Market Megamergers

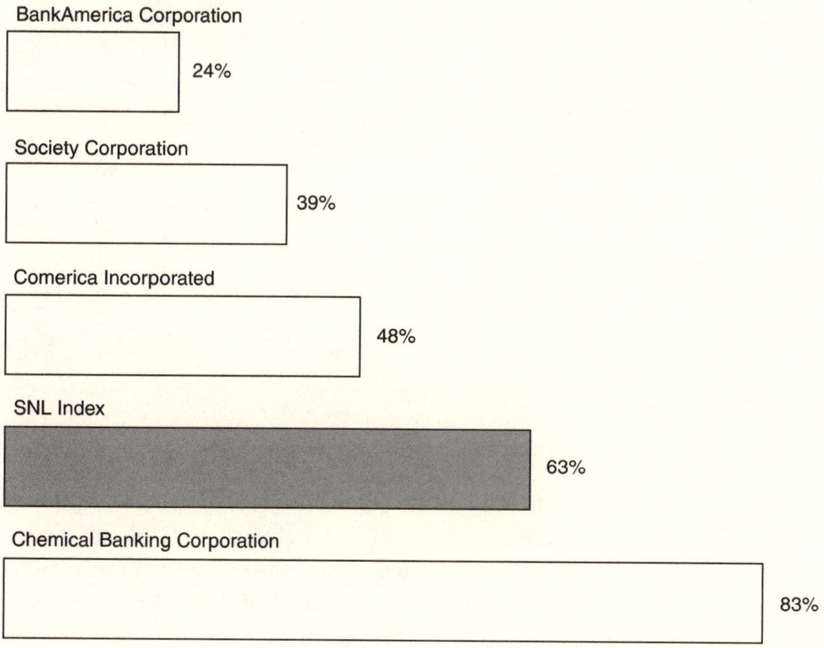

BankAmerica Corporation
24%

Society Corporation
39%

Comerica Incorporated
48%

SNL Index
63%

Chemical Banking Corporation
83%

Source: SNL Securities.

TABLE 4.2

Stock Market Reaction to Banking's Biggest Mergers

Buyer	Seller	Announcement Date	Market-Adjusted Stock Exchange (%)
BankAmerica	Security Pacific	12/08/91	16.39
Comerica	Manufacturers National	28/10/91	13.26
Chemical Banking	Manufacturers Hanover	15/07/91	12.40
Washington Mutual	Pacific First Financial	27/10/92	11.01
NationsBank	MNC Financial	18/02/93	2.67
Banc One	Team	23/03/92	−0.49
Banc One	Firstier Financial	19/04/93	−0.73
Banc One	Key Centurion	05/06/92	−1.40
Bank of New York	National Community Banks	29/01/93	−1.96
First Bank System	Colorado National	09/11/92	−2.29
First Union	Dominion	21/09/92	−3.83
KeyCorp	Puget Sound	09/03/92	−4.71
First of America	Security	12/09/91	−5.46
NBD	INB Financial	18/03/92	−5.53
Wachovia	South Carolina National	24/06/91	−5.66
(Keycorp)	(Society)	04/10/93	−6.59
NCNB	C&S/Sovran	22/07/91	−7.83
Banc One	Valley National Corp	14/04/92	−7.90
Society	AmeriTrust	13/09/91	−9.07
Marshall & Ilsley	Valley Bancorp	20/09/93	−9.87
Barnett Banks	First Florida Banks	18/05/92	−10.45
National City	Merchants National	30/10/91	−11.02
		Median	**−4.27**

Source: American Banker, November 17 1993.

In a review of all the relevant research, and all bank mergers between 1982 and 1986, Arruna Srinivasan and Larry Wall of the Federal
Reserve Bank of Atlanta found that acquiring banks were more efficient
than the industry average prior to a merger, but lost their advantage

thereafter (their noninterest expense/assets ratio actually grew faster than that of the industry as a whole).[6] Although the authors found that in-market mergers could have a significant cost impact, they concluded that "the results provide no support for the hypothesis that the typical bank merger reduces operating costs."

The difficulty with interpreting the stock market and academic responses to bank combinations lies in separating the intrinsic potential of consolidation for cost reduction and repricing from the demonstrated failure of many transactions to realize this potential (evincing once again the absence of the will and the skill to integrate effectively).

There are examples of exceptionally successful consolidation efforts. Consider two examples analyzed in an insightful review by Edward Dillon of SNL Securities, Charlottesville, Virginia.[7] Dillon sought to break out net operating expenses—recurring noninterest expense less noninterest income—to measure a merger's effect on both costs and fee income. This analysis shows the distinct sources of rapid consolidation impact for two of the leading in-market mergers of the 1980s—Wells Fargo's merger with Crocker National Corporation and Bank of New York's acquisition of Irving Bank Corporation (see Table 4.3).

In each example the acquirer's ratio of net operating expenses to average assets declined during the period spanning the calendar year before deal completion to the calendar year thereafter.

Bank of New York slashed its net operating expenses to 1.1 percent of average assets, a reduction of 42 basis points. Wells Fargo cut its ratio by 25 basis points to 2.1 percent of average assets.

Wells and Bank of New York took different routes to early success in the consolidation game.

The Wells Fargo/Crocker merger exemplified the cost rationale most often offered for in-market acquisitions, where the acquirer seeks to close overlapping branches and consolidate back-office functions. Wells reduced its pro forma noninterest expense base by about $240 million (net of restructuring, other real estate owned and amortization expenses), while

---

6   Arruna Srinivasan and Larry D. Wall, *Cost Savings Associated with Bank Mergers*, Federal Reserve Bank of Atlanta, February 1992.

7   Edward Dillon, "A Better Gauge of Merger Success: Looking at Net Operating Expenses," *American Banker*, December 8, 1993.

TABLE 4.3

Two Successful Consolidations

		Bank of New York Irving Bank 1987	Wells Fargo Crocker National 1985
Acquirer		Bank of New York	Wells Fargo
Purchased		Irving Bank	Crocker National
Year		1987	1985
B E F O R E	Joint net operating expense*	$691 million	$1,185 million
	Combined average assets	$46.6 billion	$49.6 billion
	Net operating expenses/ average assets	1.48%	2.39%
A F T E R	Joint net operating expense**	$524 million	$948 million
	Combined average assets	$49.3 billion	$44.4 billion
	Net operating expenses/ average assets	1.06%	2.14%
Net cost savings		$167 million (24.17%)	$237 million (20%)
Basis-point change in net expense ratio		−42	−25

* Recurring noninterest income less recurring noninterest expense in full calendar year preceding the merger.
** For the first full calendar year following the merger.
Source: SNL Securities.

maintaining its noninterest income at about $480 million. The result was a drop in the company's net operating expenses, from almost $1.2 billion in 1985 to just under $950 million in 1987, resulting in a 25-basis-point improvement in its ratio of net operating expenses to average assets.

Although Bank of New York also enjoyed a reduction in its expense base after the Irving acquisition of $84 million, its success was equally driven by an increase in noninterest income of $83 million, thanks to Irving's strong trust business. This generated an overall 42-basis-point improvement in its ratio of net operating expenses to average assets.

The Bank of New York/Irving and Wells Fargo/Crocker transactions are examples of the significant cost and price impact that consolidation intrinsically permits, provided that the acquirer has done its homework on the potential of the combination, and has the determination and capability to carry through the changes it projected.

When Consolidation Will Work

The major difficulties a CEO faces, in ensuring that an acquisition will recover its purchase premium within a reasonable time frame, are how to establish up front what goals should be set for the combined institution and how to go about achieving them.

A number of preparatory analyses for, and approaches to, post-merger challenges should be addressed in order for the CEO to feel confident that he or she can reengineer the new institution.

Identify Specific Sources of Value

A common failing of acquisition evaluations is that the acquirer CEO's staff talk in generalities about the level of economic impact that the combination will provide. The due diligence process must rather be used for a specific identification and quantification of distinct areas of cost and revenue improvements; if branches overlap and are to be closed, which ones, with what level of projected account runoff and what specific staff reductions? If data centers are to be consolidated, which sites will be closed and with what buildup of staff to service the consolidated bank? This also goes for each of the staff functions of the acquired bank: legal, finance, purchasing, facilities management, and so on.

Be Prepared to Aim High

In addition, in evaluating whether an acquisition makes sense, the CEO should challenge overly-conservative estimates of economic potential. In many cases a goal of 10 percent cost reduction (and no price impact) is factored into deal assessment. A goal of 40 to 50 percent of the acquired institution's cost base and 15 to 20 percent of the combined bank's fee income is not outlandish. Setting such objectives fosters creative thinking, which is the principal driver of an effective reengineering of the combined banks.

Avoid a Marriage of Equals

Even in a merger of equals, consolidation cannot involve true equality. The CEO of the dominant partner has to be prepared to make tough decisions on the basis of imperfect information, and has to commit more time to consolidation plan execution than to plan development. The risk in bank consolidations is that the early stages of the marriage become a time of "analysis paralysis," with senior management of the two organizations jockeying for political position, and protecting the status quo. The redesigned, combined bank will not be perfect. Acknowledging this before consolidation has begun will save much time and effort.

Reengineer Rather than Integrate

Although apparently at odds with the last point, the time of consolidation is an opportunity to step back and fix the misdesign inefficiencies of both partners. This is not to say that all the best practices of each bank can be blended to form the perfect bank. Nonetheless, the CEO should be prepared to "fix the parts before forming the whole" in order to avoid grafting the dominant partner's inefficient processes and practices onto the acquired bank. This can be done in a way that captures most of the reengineering potential of each bank on a stand-alone basis, to which can be added the additional benefits of consolidation. It is a difficult task but it can be built around the approach outlined in Chapters 5 to 11

IN CONCLUSION

If this approach to merger evaluation and this mindset on postmerger management is adopted, appropriate acquisition partners for reengineering can be selected and the true economic potential of consolidation can be realized. Avoiding past consolidation failures comes down once more, as in the case with a stand-alone bank, to the existence of a fundamental will to carry through the redesign with unwavering determination and the skill to create the new bank in a way that balances radical new thinking with pragmatic organizational management. With these two characteristics, the determination of when to reengineer in a consolidation program will be as evident as in the case of the stand-alone bank.

How to Reengineer

Section One provided an overview of the historical dynamics that have led to the need for reengineering basic bank economics (the "why" of the reengineering imperative), and of the telltale signs of a reengineering opportunity (the "when" for reengineering).

Section Two will outline the basic principles of a successful bank redesign, the organizational challenges these create, a systematic approach to meeting these challenges, and the implementation focus that should dominate the overall commitment to creating the new bank.

CHAPTER 5

Basic Reengineering Principles

INTRODUCTION

The unique character of banks requires a unique approach to bank reengineering. In this chapter four crucial principles will be introduced that a bank's board and CEO should bear in mind when they reengineer their institution. They should:

- Understand the complexities of reengineering.
- Take a comprehensive, bankwide approach.
- Combine top-down and bottom-up thinking.
- Set a finite, inviolable timetable for change.

UNDERSTAND THE COMPLEXITIES OF REENGINEERING

The historical development of banks and the inherent complexity of their common cost structures and pricing variables make the reengineering of banks significantly more difficult than the forms of redesign outlined for other businesses by Hammer and Champy in *Reengineering the Corporation*.[1]

---

[1] Michael Hammer and James Champy, *Reengineering the Corporation*, HarperCollins, Harper Business Press, 1993.

FIGURE 5.1

The Reengineering Levers of Banking

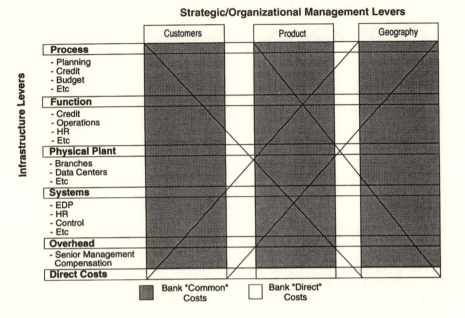

Restructuring individual processes or functions does not work in banks, as there are interdependencies within the bank both among the infrastructure levers of cost (functional, process, physical plant, and systems costs) and across strategic and organizational management levers (customer, product, and geography) for each of these sources of cost (as summarized in Figure 5.1).

A possible reengineering of small business lending, for example, might involve decentralization of responsibility to expert teams in regional branch hubs. Table 5.1 illustrates this concept. This change has considerable cascading effects on the infrastructure and management levers of the bank, as follows:

Infrastructure Levers

Process   The management of the credit origination process to ensure high underwriting standards for distributed lending, and so on.

TABLE 5.1

Possible Reengineering of Small Business Lending

Characteristic	Traditional Approach	Reengineered Approach
Delivery system	Relationship manager-based	"Hub" branch-based / National direct
Products	Multiple, tailored products	Standard "vanilla" products
Account officer responsibilities	Administration, credit, and marketing	Marketing to new and existing customers
Account loads	75 loans per account officer	350 loans per account officer
Loan approval process	Complex, individualized	Standard, automated
Documentation	Complicated, burdensome	Streamlined, automated
Turnaround time	8–10 days	1 day

Functions   The redesign of loan administration and collateral management for remote origination, servicing and workout, and so on.

Physical Plant   The implications for housing local lenders within regional branches; the creation of telecommunications between the hubs and central functional staff; creation of national, direct marketing; and so on.

Systems   The creation of EDP support systems for simplified automated credit products, incentive systems for cross-referrals, control systems for flows of paper, and electronic origination and underwriting, and so on.

Strategic and Organizational Management Levers

Customers   The management of customer relations to avoid disruption from the transfer of responsibilities; the training of account managers to handle higher account loads using new and different marketing, product, and service approaches; the removal of account officers for national, direct origination; and so on.

Product   The design of new, simplified, automated loans, the bundling of credit and liability products to ensure that deposit balances are captured from the lending relationships, and so on.

Geographic   The control of the interaction between traditional branch managers and the new hub lending teams, and between centralized wholesale lenders, administration and credit staffs, and the remote or automated originators, and so on.

This example illustrates the complex interdependencies that redesign of one business approach creates for the processes of the bank overall. A pricing change for consumer demand deposit accounts can also have unforeseen effects for critical core savings relationships and consumer credit origination.

TAKE A COMPREHENSIVE APPROACH

It is critical to look at a bank as a whole to reengineer it effectively and capitalize on the cross-bank synergies from redesign of individual processes. In the small business example above, trickle-down and trickle-up implications for cost reduction and repricing might include:

- A restructuring of wholesale lending teams at the center to reflect account load reductions and the resulting removal of the administrative burden of multiple, small-balance accounts (for credit review and approval, inquiry resolution, etc).
- The creation of separate loan documentation and collateral management units to span the wholesale, retail, and small business lines of business.
- The downsizing of existing credit and loan administration departments to reflect the standardization and automation of small credits.
- The delayering of wholesale management structures to refocus experienced salespeople on marketing to large customers rather than on administration.
- The repricing of small loans to reflect the rationalization and redesign benefits of the reengineered approach, and so on.

Many so-called reengineering projects at banks (whether internal, or in conjunction with traditional consultant approaches) fail to capitalize on the potential for interaction among bank cost levers. They take a sliver of the bank and optimize its practices, workflows, and responsibilities, without:

- Recognizing the possibilities that the redesign facilitates for improvements in related processes and systems.

◆ Understanding that this optimization may, in fact, be in direct conflict with a broader reengineering that could have far greater economic benefit for the bank overall.

◆ Capitalizing on the potential for the simplification of organizational hierarchy that is created by the simultaneous reengineering of multiple processes. (Figure 5.2 illustrates this potential.)

If senior management wishes to create a new economic structure for the late 1990s and beyond, it cannot approach reengineering as a "toe-in-the-water" exercise. A comprehensive, bankwide approach must be taken to create the opportunity for a fundamental leap in the design of processes, practices, systems, and business approaches.

Moreover, an added advantage of this principle of reengineering is that it harnesses the maximum organizational commitment to, and energy for, basic change. It clearly indicates to employees that the restructuring is a one-time process, not the first of successive dips into cost reduction following a management knee-jerk reaction to short-term earnings fluctuations. Bank of America's series of staff reductions—20,000 following the acquisition of Security Pacific, and a further 3,700 a year later after weak third-quarter 1993 results—is a good example of the latter. Staff morale can be managed through a commitment to a positive, one-time retooling of the whole organization. Double- or triple-dipping destroys faith in management, employees' enthusiasm for change and the market's sense that the bank has a clear strategic direction.

COMBINE TOP-DOWN AND BOTTOM-UP THINKING

Given the complex interdependencies in banks, neither senior management nor staff down the line can reengineer a bank alone. Fundamental direction concerning overall business management, risk management, systems and network architecture, organizational structure, and so on must come from senior management. Redesign of tasks in proof, adjustment, processing, and data storage and dissemination for check operations; in specifications development, programming, and maintenance for systems; and in mail sorting, distribution, and collection must come from the troops in the functional trenches. Although it is an overused expression, they must be "empowered" to create change. Effective reengineering has to combine

FIGURE 5.2

Organizational Hierarchy and reengineering

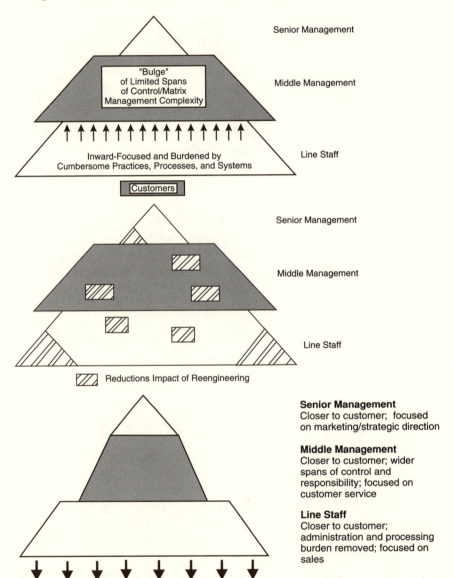

Senior Management

Middle Management

Line Staff

"Bulge"
of Limited Spans
of Control/Matrix
Management Complexity

Inward-Focused and Burdened by
Cumbersome Practices, Processes, and Systems

Customers

Senior Management

Middle Management

Line Staff

Reductions Impact of Reengineering

Senior Management
Closer to customer; focused
on marketing/strategic direction

Middle Management
Closer to customer; wider
spans of control and
responsibility; focused on
customer service

Line Staff
Closer to customer;
administration and processing
burden removed; focused on
sales

Customers

leadership from senior management on radical new approaches to the bank's direction with a mandate for redesign of basic practices, workflows, and responsibilities from the bottom-up.

SET A FINITE, INVIOLABLE TIMETABLE

If the entire bank is to be reengineered with regard to both process cost and pricing, and with both top-down and bottom-up thinking, it is often asked whether the exercise will be indeterminate in duration. It cannot be. Reengineering inevitably involves diversion of senior management's time from day-to-day direction of the bank, considerable anxiety for the staff, and disruption (although managed and controlled) of market focus.

There has to be a light at the end of the tunnel to prevent organizational paralysis. If employees are reassured that the reengineering will be completed within a reasonable time frame, they can be carefully managed to maintain a customer service focus, loyalty to the bank, and their personal health and integrity.

Of course, this requires an extremely disciplined, structured approach to reengineering, as will be outlined in Chapters 6 to 12. However, it is achievable.

In the reengineering of CoreStates Financial Corporation, Philadelphia, the overall redesign of the bank was carried out by 25 full-time and 100 part-time participants at upper and middle levels of management over a nine-month period. This time frame covered the entire reengineering design from its kickoff to the announcement of staff implications on a specific position-by-position basis. Over 12 months, CoreStates' efficiency ratio improved from 60 percent to 54 percent. Table 5.2 is a day-to-day reengineering timetable for one month of the process.

Any bank board and CEO contemplating reengineering owes it to the bank's customers and employees to ensure that reengineering does not become an indeterminate process, itself a burden on staff time and an excuse for continued inward focus.

TABLE 5.2

Working Team and Group Leader Calendar

Monday	Tuesday	Wednesday	Thursday	Friday	Saturday/Sunday
1 Step 1. Kickoff to GLs; GLs review requested revisions to base budget with finance department	**2** Step 1. GL Training	**3** Step 1. GL training (optional); Base budgets due from finance department; Consolidation methodologies due from FHs	**4**	**5** WT meeting 8:00–9:00 AM; Forms 1–4 and organization charts due from GLs; Final GL information requests due from FHs	**6** **7**
8 Step 2. Kickoff to WT; Information requests distributed to GLs	**9** Step 2. WT Training	**10**	**11** Forms 1–11 and diskettes due from GLs	**12** WT meeting 8:00–9:30 AM; Information requests due from GLs; Organization charts due from WT; Profitability analyses due from finance department; Step 2. Kickoff books to printer	**13** **14**
15 Step 2. Kickoff to GLs; Step 1. Summary materials distributed to WT	**16** Step 2. GL training	**17** Brainstorming sessions; FHs present buildup organization and group allocations to MC	**18** Brainstorming sessions	**19** WT meeting 8:00 AM–5:30 PM; Brainstorming sessions; Final buildup organization and group allocations due from FHs	**20** **21**
22 Brainstorming sessions; Buildup allocations sent to GLs	**23** Brainstorming sessions; Step 1. Summary book due	**24** Brainstorming sessions; WT presents step 1 summary to MC 1:00–3:00 PM	**25** Brainstorming sessions; Forms 12–17 and diskettes due from GLs	**26** WT meeting 8:00–11:00 AM; Brainstorming sessions; Forms 12 distributed to S/U/Rs	**27** **28**
29 Brainstorming sessions	**30** Brainstorming sessions; Step 2. Summary book due	**31** Brainstorming sessions; WT presents Step 2 summary to MC, 2:00–4:30 PM	**1** Forms 12–17 and diskettes due from GLs	**2** WT meeting 8:00–9:30 AM; Forms 12 distributed to S/U/Rs	**3** **4**

GL = Group leader   WT = Working team   MC = Management committee   FH = Functional head

CHAPTER 6

Creating Organizational Energy for Change

INTRODUCTION

Reengineering a bank is about organizational revitalization and beginning a cultural change process as much as it is about redesigning cost processes, systems, and structures, or establishing pricing discipline and outward focus. It is about the management of change. In each bank I have helped to reengineer there has been a pent-up drive among most employees to return to their raison d'être: customer focus.

Employees often know that many of the tasks they perform each day—ostensibly to serve overall processes and systems—are grossly inefficient or completely worthless. A question I normally ask of middle managers and line staff at the start of a reengineering effort is: "Would you have been proud to have returned home yesterday and told your spouse in detail how you spent your day and what you accomplished?" It is astounding—and sad—how few employees are able to answer in the affirmative. The key issue, therefore, becomes how to motivate and channel a latent desire for change into creative thinking.

Establishing the organizational context for reengineering is as important as, if not more important than, providing a structured, managed approach to harness the bank's inherent appetite for change. To this end, three organizational imperatives for successful reengineering will be outlined before discussing *how* to reengineer, *all* of which must be addressed before the bank is ready to face the redesign challenge:

- ◆ Demonstrate a commitment to change.
- ◆ Demonstrate a commitment to fairness.
- ◆ Demonstrate a commitment to involvement.

COMMITMENT TO CHANGE

Many restructuring programs do not work. In a survey by Wyatt Company,[1] 85 percent of respondents had instituted some form of corporate redesign to improve profits. After two years, in 46 percent of the cases, costs had failed to decline or, in some instances, had even risen. In addition, 58 percent of respondents had sought to increase productivity through a "restructuring," but only one-third of these achieved this goal within two years. McKinsey & Co completed a study of reengineering projects in 100 companies around the world. The McKinsey consultants found that reengineering generally did not meet the initial expectations for improvements in financial performance. Of the 20 companies studied in depth, most did not achieve cost reductions of even 13 percent in the reengineered business unit. In particular, many reengineering projects focused on reducing the costs of tasks and, therefore, failed to create improvements in processes.[2]

The cost to an organization for a failed effort is high, resulting in lower employee morale, a "restructuring-of-the-month" attitude, and a belief by many analysts and investors that management has no clear direction for the bank.

One of the primary reasons for this lack of success is a failure to involve the whole organization in the program. Line staff may follow top-down dictates for a brief period of time in the hope that management will quickly turn its attention to other matters. Also, cost-cutting or productivity-enhancing measures imposed from on high tend to breed resentment in employees who may believe the root of the problem lies in areas other than those which managements have targeted.

An organizational reengineering which involves employees from all levels within the bank commits each employee to change, thereby significantly increasing the success rate of the effort. Employees are much more likely to see the redesign as a permanent change in the way business is conducted if management truly demonstrates its commitment of the organization's valuable time and resources.

---

1   *Wall Street Journal,* December 6, 1993.
2   Gene Hall, Jim Rosenthal and Judy Wade, "How to Make Reengineering Really Work," *Harvard Business Review,* November/December 1993.

FIGURE 6.1

Layered Team Structure

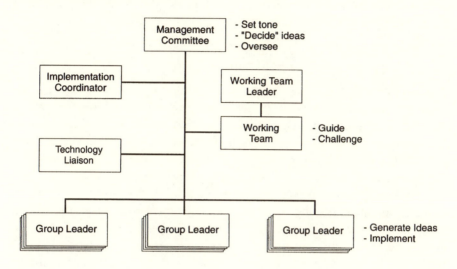

The layered team structure shown in Figure 6.1 helps illustrate the devotion to change, commitment of top management time and focus, and involvement of senior staff members and the organization as a whole. Let us look at the selection process for participants in the program, as well as their roles and functions.

Management Committee

The management committee comprises the bank's senior executives and is led by the CEO. The role of this committee throughout the reengineering is to set the tone for the program and lead it within the organization. This requires that senior managers participate actively in establishing the big "themes" for change to be investigated, and understand every detail of what the organization will undergo, both logistically and emotionally, during the course of the reengineering.

To demonstrate the bank's commitment, the management committee's focus must be very visible to all levels of staff. Specifically, members of the management committee act as the spokespersons for the effort. They actively participate in the development and delivery of:

- An internal communications program presented generally to all employees, but aimed particularly at key thought leaders.
- An external communications plan aimed at winning the support of the media and the investment community alike.

Working Team Leader

The working team leader is typically a member of the management committee, and a full 100 percent of his or her time is devoted to ensuring the success of the program. The active participation of one of the bank's most senior managers serves to instill in the other program participants, as well as in the rest of the organization, a sense of the importance and urgency that the management committee places on the reengineering.

A key role of the working team leader is to set a tone of creative thinking and radical change for the overall effort. He or she acts to eliminate any political roadblocks that might normally impede this type of progress and motivate the other program participants. In addition, the working team leader is ideally positioned to detect strategic-level concerns and morale issues as they develop, and to communicate such potential problems to the management committee in a timely manner. Last, the working team leader serves as the "point person" for the concerns of participants and other employees.

Any change process within an organization inevitably creates uncertainty and apprehension. With this in mind, the working team leader acts as an emotional sounding board—alternatively guiding, challenging, and reassuring staff to continue moving the program toward its goal.

Working Team

By challenging supervisory-level managers (the "group leaders") to stretch their thinking and become aggressive in their approach, the working team plays a critical role in guiding the process.

The management committee selects 10 to 30 individuals to serve as full-time members of this team, depending on the size of the bank. As shown in Figure 6.2 approximately three-quarters of the working team focus on the process redesign side. The remainder tackle pricing and cross-bank expenses (taking a "horizontal" look at each line item expense to complement group leaders' "vertical" perspective on their particular organizational or functional areas).

FIGURE 6.2

Working Team Structure

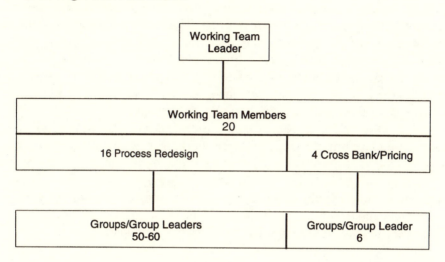

Because it examines all areas of the bank, the working team should represent a mix of people from all parts of the organization, including retail, wholesale, trust, systems, operations, and administration. A majority of the working team is ideally drawn from line areas, with approximately 10 percent pulled from staff departments. More importantly, the team members are assigned to review areas of the bank outside their normal realm of responsibility. This helps give a new sense of perspective to the functional area and minimizes the politics surrounding ideas for change. A working team member from operations may, for example, be able to apply a workflow process analysis to the way in which audits are performed. The goal is to produce a more radical redesign; a means of doing better things, rather than doing the same things in a better way.

Because the working team plays such an active role in the process, the selection of team members is critical. Primarily, they should be senior-level managers who lead by example, rather than by command, and who can create an environment that is conducive to change.

Second, working team members should have a proven track record: they should be top performers that the bank "cannot spare."

The third important characteristic is rigorous analytical skills. Members of the working team should be those with an ability to anticipate, as well as solve, problems, and those who are willing to take the time required to understand the details of an issue.

Last, they should be good team players. The collaborative nature of the reengineering process, the time invested by senior management and the emotions generated by uncertainty necessitate the selection of individuals who will value the contributions of each participant and encourage active involvement. When helping a bank to reengineer, I spend one or two days with the management committee, using the work sheet in Figure 6.3, to ensure that real "change agents" are selected for the working team.

In order to truly divorce them from their day-to-day responsibilities and to build a spirit of camaraderie, the working team members are moved out of their traditional offices and placed in a "bull pen" environment (a collection of desks, rather than separate offices) for the duration of the reengineering program. This strategy helps demonstrate the importance of teamwork and facilitates the exchange of information among working team members, across groups, and with the working team leader.

Group Leaders

A group represents the basic unit of the reengineering effort that will analyze current processes and tasks, and generate ideas for change. Groups do not have to reflect either the existing or the future organizational structure of the bank. Rather, they are formed from "responsibility centers" on the basis of the fact that their members serve similar processes, functions, or markets.

The group leader is a manager of one of the responsibility centers constituting the group. Group leaders spend approximately 75 percent of their time on the reengineering process, and more during peak periods. They are responsible for gathering, analyzing, inputting, improving upon, and presenting the data required for reengineering, and for leading their units in developing creative redesign approaches to business operations. At the conclusion of the effort the group leaders are often also responsible for implementing the decisions reached by the management committee and are held accountable for the process and economic impact of each idea. They should be selected, therefore, on the basis of their attention to detail and their demonstrated responsibility, as well as for their creativity and their organizational talents. The management committee spends many hours selecting the best candidates for group leaders.

FIGURE 6.3

Selection Criteria

Candidate	Track Record	Leadership Skill	Team Player	Analytical Skill	Total Score	Decision
T Jones	4	3	4	3	14	Yes
B Murphy	4	2	3	4	13	Yes
K Smith	3	3	2	3	11	No
J Cespedes	3	4	4	3	14	Yes
J Vander	4	4	4	2	14	Yes
A Simon	4	3	4	3	14	Yes
D Young	3	3	4	4		
M Curran	3	3	4			
L Moore	3	3				
K Pe	3					

Rate each candidate using the following scale:

4 Exceptional
3 Good
2 Average
1 Below average

101

Implementation Coordinators

The implementation coordinators are one or two members of the working team who are most actively involved in setting up the program before it commences and in facilitating and tracking the results of the reengineering during its implementation. The primary roles of the implementation co-ordinators are to facilitate the mechanics of the process and to monitor the integrity of execution.

Technology Liaison Team

The technology liaison team acts as a resource to the group leaders and working team. In addition to reviewing the cost estimates for those ideas requiring automation, the team proactively brings ideas to the attention of group leaders and the working team about automation opportunities within and across all groups, and helps brainstorm new technology opportunities within a group.

Advantages of Structure

The advantages of using this layered team structure to drive the reengineering effort are threefold. First, it creates a direct line between the management committee and supervisory-level managers, allowing for a two-way flow of information and ideas, and thereby overcoming traditional barriers to change that derive from the complex bulge of middle management in banks. Second, it takes highly creative change agents away from the safety of their line or staff positions and challenges them to think from scratch, looking at areas where they have no vested political interest to protect. Last, it shows that senior management is committed to looking at all areas of the bank, with no holds barred.

Many managers have stated that their involvement in this team environment was the most intense, exciting opportunity of their careers to date, and that the sense of freedom it helped create carried over into their subsequent work habits. In one case, the working team continued to meet every couple of months—even after two years—to brainstorm new ways of doing better things.

COMMITMENT TO FAIRNESS

The commitment of the bank's resources to change—in terms of finances and personnel—is a powerful signal. Of equal importance, however, is whether employees perceive that management is being as fair as it can in carrying out the program.

In banking it is a simple fact that staff equals cost, given the high levels of personnel expense. Some layoffs are therefore inevitable. But employee anxiety can be controlled and staff commitment maintained if it is felt that the reengineering is something that everyone in the bank faces together, and that whatever can be done to ease human resources issues will be done. The following two approaches should be employed.

Nonarbitrary Approach

The commitment to fairness begins with an evaluation of every area and every process within the bank. To exclude any group from review would be perceived as giving it special treatment, no matter how valid the reason for the exclusion. This would be particularly sensitive if the group were the responsibility of an influential manager. No process or business should be reserved as a sacred cow (i.e., something that cannot be touched or altered). A commitment to fairness implies that management believes every aspect of the bank has the potential to be redesigned in a more efficient manner.

Involving all areas of the bank, however, although necessary, is not of itself sufficient. The crucial issue is how each area is involved in the program. Many restructuring programs apply a random, across-the-board cost reduction requirement to all departments without regard to their existing status. The true reengineering of an institution requires a thoughtful review of every area of the bank, the establishment of aggressive cost-reduction targets for each; and, most important, a recognition of the risk associated with every new idea. As a result, each group will be affected differently by the ultimate redesign, reflecting its past management effectiveness and its future role in the strategy of the bank.

This type of nonarbitrary approach cannot be implemented immediately. It takes a true time commitment to develop and evaluate the options available to the bank. The core benefit of such an approach, however, is that it creates a permanent annuity impact on costs and revenues. This differs substantially from the usual restructuring program, in which costs tend to creep back over time.

Comprehensive Human Resources Strategy

From the human resources perspective, reengineering becomes a huge challenge, both in terms of the magnitude of the change and the scope of the bankwide effort. For legal reasons, as well as for the sake of employee morale, it is essential that the human resources process be conducted in the most equitable manner possible.

The reengineering program focuses initially on eliminating ineffective and redundant processes, rather than on eliminating individuals. Once the layout of the redesigned organization has been determined, however, a seamless approach has to be in place for identifying affected staff members. After this process is complete, the organization must turn its attention to gaining the re-commitment of remaining staff, and the re-energizing of the organization.

Recruitment Freeze

A recruitment freeze, imposed at the beginning of the project, is an important component in providing fairness in the human resources plan for two primary reasons. First, the positions that will be needed in the redesigned organization have not yet been defined. Hiring new staff for unfilled positions in a certain department at the beginning of the process signals to the organization that perhaps that department is not to be affected. In any event, newly hired personnel could find their positions eliminated weeks or months after they have been hired. Second, to provide those employees who are released as a result of the reengineering with the greatest opportunity to find another position within the bank, unfilled positions should be left open until the end of the project. If they are then still needed, filling them with the bank's current employees is an outstanding way to demonstrate loyalty to those who worked so diligently to create the new organization.

Promotions and Salary Freeze

Similar logic should be applied to promotions and pay increases. As these are often viewed as a reward for meritorious performance, it can be perceived as exceedingly unjust to provide employees with a pat on the back one week, then release them the next.

Moreover, even if a position is not eliminated, it may undergo dramatic change from the redesign. The new demands of the position may require employees of lower or higher salary grade. In order to minimize uncertainty and confusion, promotions and changes in compensation are best frozen until the conclusion of the project.

Employee Selection

One of the most difficult decisions of a reengineering is to determine how employees are to be selected for release or retention. Should the selection be based on tenure, skills, or past performance? How can this process ever truly be fair? Although released staff may judge whichever method was chosen to have been biased, an equitable selection process should be established at the start of the project and applied consistently.

There are several selection policy options. One of the simplest methods to determine which individuals will be released is "as it falls." In this approach, the person in the eliminated position is released, regardless of his or her level of performance or length of tenure. The benefit of this method is that it is easily defensible from a legal perspective. However, the significant drawback is that the bank could unnecessarily lose some of its very best people.

A second option is to base selection on service tenure. Eliminating individuals on the basis of seniority is easily administered and objective, and, therefore, it involves low litigation risk. If consistently applied, however, this method does not allow management any discretion in the decision-making process.

A more complex approach is to take the reengineering as an opportunity to upgrade the bank's skill levels and eliminate lower-level performers. This can be accomplished through a variety of methods. For example, the top performers in positions to be eliminated could be swapped with the worst performers in retained positions.

Alternatively, a pool could be created for the top 20 percent of performers. Although this approach has the benefit of allowing the bank to retain its best employees, there are some serious implementation considerations. First, the bank must establish a standard of measurement. Past employee reviews are insufficient indicators of performance because there is often a great deal of inconsistency among supervisors and departments in their performance ratings. Also, past performance may not be indicative of a match with the skills needed in the redesigned organization.

A skills- and values-based assessment is a selection method which evaluates individuals against the skills required to perform the job. It involves a three-step approach:

- Defining the skills and abilities needed to carry out the responsibilities of the new position and to implement the emerging values of the new organization.
- Gathering information and evaluating the skills of the existing talent pool and its fit with the new values.
- Selecting the best-qualified employees on the basis of their fit with the skills and the new values required by the new organization. This method, although the most complex, offers the

greatest advantages to the organization. The approach is consistent with that used by managers in the hiring process, and it prepares the organization to meet the needs of the future. Since this procedure is potentially very time-consuming, care should be taken to develop a simplified methodology and to begin the assessments as early as possible. An outline to the approach is illustrated in Figure 6.4.

In practice, a combination of these methods is often the most appropriate choice. Skills- and values-based assessments are particularly important for higher personnel grades and may be applied to all exempt employees (i.e., those not subject to the wage and overtime provisions of the relevant labor legislation). The assessments are, however, fairly laborious and, because the skills required for nonexempt employees are unlikely to change dramatically, performance-based or tenure-based selection criteria are often the most efficient methods to use for nonexempt personnel.

An option which discriminates among employees, on whatever basis, is wrong and open to legal challenge. Selection based upon performance requires solid documentation and a review of the cumulative effect of ultimate decisions to ensure that no one category of employees is treated unfairly relative to others.

In any case, no selection criterion will prevent the bank from losing some good performers. It is very difficult to match the process of selectively releasing poor performers with eliminating identified positions. It is important, therefore, that managers do not make the promise that all the best people will find a position with the bank after the redesign is complete. As reengineering necessarily involves radical change in the demands on staff, even some employees who were considered superior performers in the past will simply not fit into the new world.

Timing of Notifications

Not every position scheduled for elimination can be removed immediately. Many ideas will be phased in over a year to 18 months. The timing of employee notifications therefore becomes an issue. One option is to notify the affected employees during the month or quarter in which their positions are to be eliminated. The benefit of this approach is that it creates maximum flexibility to control and reduce severance costs. However, it also creates an environment of uncertainty. All employees are concerned about the safety of their positions as each notification period begins. Rumors begin to circulate, and employees are often distracted by concerns about their

FIGURE 6–4

Skills-Based Selection Principles

1. Select the best employee for the job and fit with the bank's emerging values. It is essential that all selections be made in a nondiscriminatory manner.

2. In making the employee selections, it is not necessary to have equal representation from each affiliate, for the sake of balancing alone. However, good business sense would indicate that a balanced team is appropriate in some cases.

3. Make a strong effort to get to know all candidates. Give candidates from all affiliate banks equal consideration. Be careful not to follow biases arising from long-time associations.

4. Ensure that the employees selected have the required skills and values to perform the job in the new organization.

5. Review of past performance is a secondary consideration to be viewed in the context of the skill requirements for the future position.

6. Consider the recommendation of the manager with direct responsibility for the position. The final decisions should not be made without the input of the direct manager.

7. Consider the input on the candidates' skills from many sources, not just their current manager. Also, ask candidates to supply information on themselves and their backgrounds.

8. Identify the functional skills/abilities needed for each position clearly. These skills should match the future business needs of the area.

9. Consider candidate input and preference where possible.

10. Where the skills-based review produces a "tie," seniority will serve as a tiebreaker for the selection decision.

11. All selections should be reviewed prior to communication to employees to ensure that aggregate selections across the corporation comply with the spirit of the organization's affirmative action program.

future. Without an extremely effective communications plan, the bank is likely to lose some of its best performers as uncertainty causes them to look outside the organization for new jobs.

Notifying all affected employees on a single day eliminates this uncertainty. It introduces an additional concern, however. How can critical positions, which will be eliminated perhaps six or nine months later, be protected in the interim? One solution is to award performance bonuses to people in critical jobs. This option must be used very selectively, however, or it can reduce the control of separation costs. Another way to protect critical positions is to create understudies, so as to temporarily staff the positions with individuals who will remain with the organization. This option requires a careful assessment of which jobs are truly critical to the organization.

A third option is to combine the two approaches to the timing of notifications. All affected exempt employees (for whom there is relatively low turnover) are notified on the same day, regardless of when their positions are scheduled to be eliminated. This reduces uncertainty and ensures that the bank does not lose people that it wants to retain. On the other hand, affected nonexempt employees are not notified until the month in which the releases are scheduled to occur. The rationale behind this treatment of nonexempt employees is that, with a relatively high turnover, positions may be eliminated automatically through attrition without requiring formal separations of existing employees. This combined approach has the advantages of preserving a degree of control over severance costs, dealing with employees fairly by avoiding unnecessary pain, and reducing risks to the bank.

Severance Policy

The parameters of the bank's severance policies must be set in the context of the reengineering effort, local employment levels, and the skills of the individuals involved. The existing severance program could be enhanced through an "early-out" program. Banks should not implement a comprehensive early retirement plan, however, as these often induce the wrong people to leave and increase severance costs substantially. A less expensive alternative, from both a fiscal and an organizational standpoint, is to offer early-outs selectively to people with special needs. Nonetheless, this must be applied in a consistent manner to be legally defensible.

In addition to severance decisions, the bank must also determine how much outplacement support to provide. Outplacement services can be provided either by the bank's own human resources department or by specialized outplacement firms. Cost is generally the determining factor.

One relatively inexpensive form of outplacement service which the organization can provide is active job-search assistance by the management committee and other senior managers to whom the individuals have reported. These managers can provide contacts and references which acknowledge that the redesign of the organization necessarily resulted in layoffs, rather than reflecting the performance of the affected individuals.

Although severance costs are obviously dependent upon the level of benefits granted, it should be emphasized that severance situations typically represent only a small fraction of the total freed positions identified. Moreover, they can explicitly be managed down by instituting a recruitment freeze, accelerating the timing of some notifications, delaying the timing of other releases, and allowing selective, voluntary elections. Other ways to reduce severance costs include combining severance or outplacement with part-time work and actively searching for redeployment opportunities. Although these choices seek to grant employees additional options, while reducing overall costs to the bank, care must be taken to avoid unnecessary redeployment or part-time jobs, which again could defeat the redesign effort.

Re-commitment of the Organization

Human resources programs do not end with the reengineering implementation. Rather, it is also critical to achieve the re-commitment of those employees who remain with the organization. The bank needs to plan activities that boost morale and build the team spirit of retained staff. Because the displacement process may last from 12 to 18 months, the message that the bank is better equipped to meet the challenges of the future needs to be continually reinforced. In many ways, this process of recapturing the "hearts and minds" of employees is the most important component of successful redesign.

COMMITMENT TO INVOLVEMENT

Involving the entire organization in what is perceived as a high-priority and fair process helps create an environment in which employees believe in the change process, participate in the way that their respective processes and activities are redesigned, and possess a sense of ownership of the changes implemented.

Involving the entire organization in redesigning the institution, however, takes time and commitment on the part of senior management. Furthermore, a process must be devised to allow all employees a voice, enabling them to sense that their contributions are valued. This requires a creative approach to communicating to, and soliciting ideas from, all staff members.

Communications Process

The goals of a structured, continuous communications process are to promote a true sense of participation among employees and to keep all the bank's constituencies informed about the progress and developments of the reengineering program. Several steps are integral to designing communications that successfully accomplish these goals.

Set an Economic/Project Rationale

The economic or project rationale conveys the purpose for undertaking such a radical institutional reengineering. The rationale is communicated to both internal and external constituencies and, therefore, should be honest but upbeat. A good example of a rationale statement from one reengineering program went as follows:

> Only the best, most efficient banks will be able to survive increased competition from banks and nonbanks offering financial services in the 1990s. In order to satisfy shareholder demands, raise additional capital in the equity markets and keep pace with ever-changing technology, [the bank] will have to improve dramatically its financial performance. Keys to this strategy of enhancing financial performance are: (1) improvement of profit margins through revenue growth, and (2) effective redesign of business processes. This process will be accomplished in a participatory manner with input and assistance from all levels of employees within the organization.

Select a Name for the Process

As with any team, a name serves as a rallying point for its supporters. The name should be simple, yet describe the project to larger audiences. Examples of some project names that have been used effectively in the past include: "A Plus," "Best," "Excel," "Advance," and "Vision."

Actively Direct Internal Communications

One of the most important considerations is to determine what will be communicated to each staff level within the bank. The first set of individuals who become aware of the process (outside of senior management) is the working team. A means of effectively (and enthusiastically) communicating the start-up of the project, providing an overview of the approach, and announcing the selection of the working team members is essential to generating excitement for the redesign effort. Selection of the working team, in particular, can be positioned as recognition of the stature of its members, as well as of the project overall.

Senior and middle-level managers who are not part of the working team must also be informed and involved. These managers will have a number of questions regarding the scope of the project, their roles, the implications for their areas of responsibility, and the human resources issues that will develop. Communicating with these key thought leaders is necessary to gain their support early on. Although these managers do not participate in the project on a day-to-day basis, they can have a dramatic influence on the way that their subordinates and the entire organization perceive it.

Careful attention must be paid to the manner in which these managers are informed. A general meeting, followed by one-to-one discussions between select managers and the management committee, can help alleviate fears and silence any potential squeaky wheels. In addition, sending each manager a written invitation to the initial meeting is a way of conferring a sense of distinction and involvement.

Last, the management committee has to craft the general message to be delivered to all the bank's employees. The message should be broad enough to give each staff member an accurate picture of the program that will be carried out within the organization, while omitting a level of detail that would generate confusion and unnecessary uncertainty. Senior managers should also provide a more personal level of communication. Department meetings should be held to supplement the general announcement and answer the myriad of questions that employees will raise. An open and honest approach, consistently applied, is the best means to involve employees at all organizational levels. Staff members are quick to see through half-truths and platitudes.

After the program's initial commencement, regular communication updates should be used to ensure the continuing involvement of all employees. These updates can take the form of a project newsletter, posters, memorandums from the working team, and so on. Informing all employees of how the project is progressing and the steps that remain to be accomplished contributes to a sense of participation and certainty. It is impossible to communicate too much.

Determine the External Constituencies

The bank has a number of external constituencies that will be interested in the reengineering effort or may require notification. These include regulators, the media, customers, and the investment community. Although many decisions must be made with regard to how to communicate with these constituencies (for example, preemptive versus reactive communications, background material, ongoing updates, answers to commonly asked questions), perhaps the most important decision is who should be the spokesperson. Although the management committee should appoint a small communications committee to prepare and review materials designed for internal and external distribution, they should select one external spokesperson, generally a member of the management committee, for the entire project. This will ensure that all external constituencies hear a consistent, coherent and positive message concerning the redesign effort.

Human Resources Communications

The goal of the human resources communications program is to make employees aware of the steps that have been taken to make the process as fair as possible, while creating a new, re-energized organization. A critical component of a successful human resources communication effort is a clear, explicit statement of the human resources philosophy and the parameters of the program created for the redesign effort.

The most sensitive communications issues will arise with regard to employee separations. At the appropriate time, a clear policy statement should be issued and each manager should receive instructions regarding the detailed human resources process for his or her department. The training of managers is critical to the integrity of the entire human resources program. Managers must be made aware of the selection criteria and their application, as well as the legal ramifications of their choices. Specific guidelines should be issued regarding employee notification and separation procedures. The communications strategy is summarized in Figure 6.5.

Top-Down/Bottom-Up Approach

In order to keep each employee involved in the reengineering program, it cannot be driven solely from the top. The redesign approach must combine radical, comprehensive, top-down policy initiatives and process redesign themes with a thorough, bottom-up review of the bank's processes and tasks, to make implementation of appropriate radical changes a reality down the line. Employees at all levels of the organization should be encouraged to contribute, since then they will "own" implementation.

Solicitation of ideas from mid-level managers and below is effective in identifying those tasks that most frustrate employees. A bottom-up process is a means of empowering each employee to redesign his or her responsibilities in the manner that he or she would find most effective and productive.

As it would be impossible to solicit comments directly from every individual in the bank, however, other opportunities for employees to contribute should be made available. An anonymous e-mail process can be

FIGURE 6.5

Communications Outline

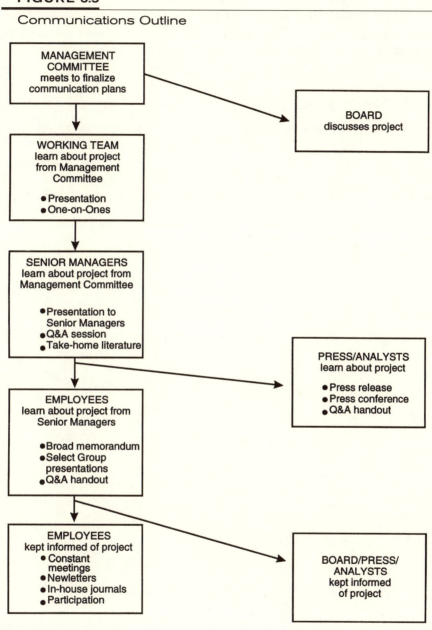

helpful in encouraging employees to participate when they might otherwise feel uncomfortable. Maintaining a telephone hot line for suggestions can accommodate those employees who need more personal contact. Yet, regardless of how employees participate, all should be made to feel that their contributions are valued.

IN CONCLUSION

It may seem odd to have covered in this chapter the commitment, fairness, and involvement issues of reengineering before explicitly reviewing how a structured approach to redesign is executed, yet this has been done deliberately. All the components described are critical for creating organizational energy for change; all must be in place before the bank is set on its reengineering course.

CHAPTER 7

A Systematic Approach to Bank Reengineering— Preparation

INTRODUCTION

Chapter 6 showed that reinvigorating the organization is at least as important as, if not more important than, providing a structured, managed approach to reengineering. Nevertheless, a formal approach to managing the involvement of the whole bank is essential.

As discussed earlier, three core principles of bank reengineering are to:

* Take a comprehensive cross-bank approach.
* Combine top-down and bottom-up thinking.
* Set a finite, inviolable timetable for the program.

Meeting the first two requirements, while still satisfying the third, is obviously a significant challenge.

Rigorous preparation, a well-oiled formal process for carrying out the project, automated support wherever possible, and clear communication of the project's day-to-day demands on participants are crucial both to achieving high quality standards in redesign and to keeping organizational disruption to a reasonable, manageable level. Moreover, senior management must carefully review any other projects already under way that may compete with the resources required for the redesign process. Decisions must be made on whether to delay or to accelerate these projects so that the organization can devote its full attention to reengineering the bank.

TABLE 7.1

The Six-Step Approach to Reengineering

Step	Major Components	Chapter
Preparation for change	**Psychological preparation** **Cost preparation** **Repricing preparation**	7
Understanding current processes	**Understanding processes and costs**	7
Understanding current pricing	**Contribution analysis** **Product workflow analysis** **Unit cost derivation** **Customer relationship analysis** **Value analysis**	7
Generating reengineering options	Top-down approaches for process cost design Top-down approaches to repricing Bottom-up approach	8
Refining options	Evaluation of the options Upgrading ideas	8
Charting the new bank's course	Planning the future Tracking achievement Avoiding execution pitfalls Re-commitment of the new bank	9

Chapters 7 to 9 describe a six-step approach to reengineering that has achieved these goals—and has done so not merely to produce short-term earnings improvement, but rather, an annuity of earnings and a lasting redirection of the market focus, service quality, resource allocations and pricing sophistication of the banks involved. These steps, as shown in Table 7.1 are:

 ◆ Preparing for change.
 ◆ Understanding current costs.
 ◆ Understanding current pricing.
 ◆ Generating reengineering options.[1]

---

1   See Chapters 8 and 9.

- ◆ Refining options.[2]
- ◆ Creating the new bank.[3]

PREPARING FOR CHANGE
Psychological Preparation

Chapter 6 described the importance of developing a communications program to ensure the involvement of the entire organization and to prepare it for the changes that will take place over the course of the reengineering effort. In introducing the reengineering to the organization, several important points must be emphasized. First, regardless of whether the organization has been an outstanding, an average, or a poor performer in the past, the industry as it will develop in the 1990s and beyond is undergoing a dramatic structural change. The program must, therefore, be framed as a positive action which is crucial to positioning the bank to meet the demands of the future. Second, each member of the organization must be challenged to redesign what he or she does each day. Last, the goals—to create a streamlined, effective organization and to ensure that all parts of the bank work together as a cohesive unit—must be stated clearly and incorporated into each aspect of communication of the effort.

Cost Preparation

After the organization is prepared psychologically for change, the project's logistics can be planned. In order to judge the effects of the reengineering, the organization has to assess where it stands. This is accomplished by preparing a baseline budget that is used as the standard against which to measure all redesign opportunities.

On the cost side, the baseline budget represents the controllable and ongoing noninterest expenses of the entire bank. The basis for the baseline budget can be the previous 12-month financial statement, annualized year-to-date results, or other similar measures. The resulting costs are then scrutinized to exclude unusual and non-recurring expenses, as well as noncontrollable expenses, such as FDIC insurance and depreciation. Also, cost reductions from independent initiatives that are already planned should be identified, quantified, and excluded from the baseline budget.

---

2   Ibid.

3   Chapter 9.

Once the overall bank's budget has been established, it must then be broken down to correspond to the individual groups. (As defined in Chapter 6, groups are a collection of responsibility centers that form the basic analytical units of the reengineering program.) For each group, expenses are divided into personnel and nonpersonnel categories. In the interest of simplicity and fairness (such as focusing on positions, rather than on specific staff members), personnel expenses are aggregated into 6 to 8 categories and nonpersonnel expenses into about 20 categories. The derivation of the baseline budget is summarized in Figure 7.1, and an example of personnel and nonpersonnel expense categories is shown in Table 7.2.

The personnel categories are determined by creating a distribution across exempt and nonexempt employees. Further distinctions are made for senior executives and for part-time employees. A sample distribution is provided in Table 7.3. The number of full-time equivalent (FTE) employees in each personnel category also becomes part of the baseline budget, and an organization chart for each group is developed to provide a starting point for subsequent redesign.

Repricing Preparation

As with expenses, a revenue baseline budget is prepared on the pricing side. This identifies the revenues generated from each of the bank's main businesses and product lines. The basis for the revenue baseline can be derived from the previous 12-month financials or from annualized year-to-date results. Revenues are examined to exclude extraordinary and nonrecurring income such as asset sales, and to identify and exclude the revenues attributable to other revenue enhancement projects under way in specific business areas or product lines.

Understanding Existing Process Costs

Before the actual redesign of the organization begins, it is necessary to understand the objectives and tasks of each group and the proportion of the bank's resources that they consume. This analysis results in a detailed breakdown of the tasks performed in each group and the processes to which these contribute. During this data-gathering phase of the program each group decides what to analyze and dissects it in minute detail, allocating personnel and nonpersonnel costs to each activity performed by the group, as illustrated in Figure 7.2.

FIGURE 7.1

Baseline Budget Derivation

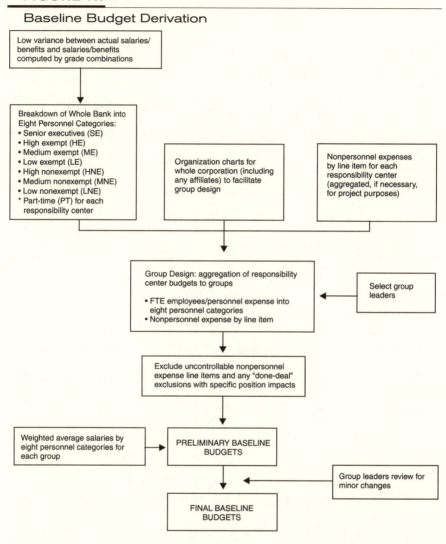

An objective answers the question why a process is performed. For example, one objective is: "To sell and/or cross-sell credit products and services to businesses." A "task" is one step in "how" this objective is achieved. Sample tasks associated with the credit sales objective might include: identifying and researching prospects; marketing credit products

TABLE 7.1

Sample Baseline Budget

Area	Group ID	Group Name	Responsibility Center Name	Resp Center	Total FTES	SE FTE	SE $	HE FTE	HE $	ME FTE	ME $	LE FTE	LE $	Total Exempt $	HNE FTE	HNE $	MNE FTE	MNE $	LNE FTE	LNE $	PT FTE	PT $	Non-exempt $
Misc.	1	Facilities		0173901	0	0	0	0	$0	0	$0	0	$0	$0	0	$0	0	$0	0	$0	0	$0	$0
Ops.	1	Facilities		0163004	9	0	0	0	$0	0	$0	1	$34	$34	1	$30	6	$145	1	$21	0	$0	$196
Ops.	1	Facilities		0165610	0	0	0	0	$0	0	$0	0	$0	$0	0	$0	0	$0	0	$0	0	$0	$0
Misc.	1	Facilities		0190815	0	0	0	0	$0	0	$0	0	$0	$0	0	$0	0	$0	0	$0	0	$0	$0
Ops.	1	Facilities		0165710	13	0	0	1	$53	0	$0	1	$35	$88	1	$28	2	$51	8	$143	0	$0	$222
Ops.	1	Facilities		0165401	0	0	0	0	$0	0	$0	0	$0	$0	0	$0	0	$0	0	$0	0	$0	$0
Ops.	1	Facilities		5553020	19	0	0	0	$0	1	$44	0	$0	$44	4	$145	13	$355	1	$24	0	$0	$524
Misc.	1	Facilities		0165901	0	0	0	0	$0	0	$0	0	$0	$0	0	$0	0	$0	0	$0	0	$0	$0
Misc.	1	Facilities		0110401	0	0	0	0	$0	0	$0	0	$0	$0	0	$0	0	$0	0	$0	0	$0	$0
Ops.	1	Facilities		0165730	17	0	0	1	$65	2	$92	2	$70	$227	2	$73	8	$174	1	$17	1	$23	$287
Misc.	1	Facilities		0136201	0	0	0	0	$0	0	$0	0	$0	$0	0	$0	0	$0	0	$0	0	$0	$0
Ops.	1	Facilities		0109201	2	0	0	0	$0	0	$0	0	$0	$0	0	$0	1	$24	0	$0	1	$19	$43
Ops.	1	Facilities		0164201	0	0	0	0	$0	0	$0	0	$0	$0	0	$0	0	$0	0	$0	0	$0	$0
Ops.	1	Facilities		0163002	17	0	0	0	$0	1	$42	0	$0	$42	1	$37	13	$318	2	$36	0	$0	$391
Misc.	1	Facilities		0164501	0	0	0	0	$0	0	$0	0	$0	$0	0	$0	0	$0	0	$0	0	$0	$0
Ops.	1	Facilities		0165202	0	0	0	0	$0	0	$0	0	$0	$0	0	$0	0	$0	0	$0	0	$0	$0
Ops.	1	Facilities		0164801	9	0	0	0	$0	0	$0	0	$0	$0	1	$42	5	$148	2	$30	2	$32	$252
Ops.	1	Facilities		0109301	0	0	0	0	$0	0	$0	0	$0	$0	0	$0	0	$0	0	$0	0	$0	$0
Ops.	1	Facilities		0163001	20	0	0	2	$145	4	$194	0	$0	$339	5	$172	8	$193	1	$23	0	$0	$388

Personnel Categories

TABLE 7.2

Concluded

Area	Group ID	Group Name	Respon-sibility Center Name	Resp Centre	Nonpersonnel Categories																		
					Total	CCR	DSB	MLO	ACC	PSS	AMS	CMP	PFS	EXS	BPC	CRH	SSV	OUT	TTT	BME	CON	GLF	OTH
Misc.	1	Facilities		0173901	0	0	0	0	0	0	0	0	0	0	0	0	0	0	0	0	0	0	0
Ops.	1	Facilities		0163004	93	12	2	0	4	10	0	7	6	10	3	0	5	8	4	10	12	0	0
Ops.	1	Facilities		0165610	0	0	0	0	0	0	0	0	0	0	0	0	0	0	0	0	0	0	0
Misc.	1	Facilities		0190815	0	0	0	0	0	0	0	0	0	0	0	0	0	0	0	0	0	0	0
Ops.	1	Facilities		0165710	101	17	3	0	1	20	0	4	5	11	3	0	5	7	3	9	13	0	0
Ops.	1	Facilities		0165401	0	0	0	0	0	0	0	0	0	0	0	0	0	0	0	0	0	0	0
Ops.	1	Facilities		5553020	52	4	0	0	0	5	0	3	3	7	4	0	4	5	3	8	6	0	0
Misc.	1	Facilities		0165901	0	0	0	0	0	0	0	0	0	0	0	0	0	0	0	0	0	0	0
Misc.	1	Facilities		0110401	0	0	0	0	0	0	0	0	0	0	0	0	0	0	0	0	0	0	0
Ops.	1	Facilities		0165730	45	8	2	0	1	6	0	4	2	1	2	0	2	2	3	5	7	0	0
Misc.	1	Facilities		0136201	0	0	0	0	0	0	0	0	0	0	0	0	0	0	0	0	0	0	0
Ops.	1	Facilities		0109201	69	20	15	0	3	7	0	3	4	6	0	0	1	2	1	3	4	0	0
Ops.	1	Facilities		0164201	0	0	0	0	0	0	0	0	0	0	0	0	0	0	0	0	0	0	0
Ops.	1	Facilities		0163002	54	10	6	0	2	5	0	5	3	5	1	0	2	2	3	4	6	0	0
Misc.	1	Facilities		0164501	0	0	0	0	0	0	0	0	0	0	0	0	0	0	0	0	0	0	0
Misc.	1	Facilities		0165202	0	0	0	0	0	0	0	0	0	0	0	0	0	0	0	0	0	0	0
Ops.	1	Facilities		0164801	71	6	7	0	2	3	0	4	8	10	3	0	4	3	4	7	10	0	0
Ops.	1	Facilities		0109301	0	0	0	0	0	0	0	0	0	0	0	0	0	0	0	0	0	0	0
Ops.	1	Facilities		0163001	80	5	13	0	3	5	0	5	7	8	2	0	3	4	5	8	12	0	0

121

TABLE 7.3

Personnel Expense

Personnel Category	Grade Levels	FTE	Salary ($000s)
Senior executive	63	8	$85+
High exempt	58–62	99	$44–119
percent of officers		30%	
Medium exempt	55–57	135	$32–63
percent of officers		39%	
Low exempt	52–54	102	$24–46
percent of officers		29%	
High nonexempt	9–13	108	$22–49
percent of staff		9%	
Medium nonxempt	5–8	556	$16–33
percent of staff		44%	
Low nonexempt	1–4	595	$13–25
percent of staff		47%	

FIGURE 7.2

Process Cost Analysis

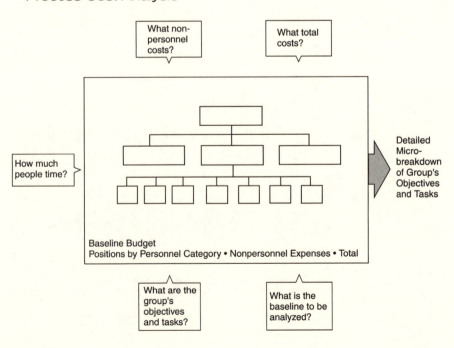

What non-personnel costs?

What total costs?

How much people time?

Detailed Micro-breakdown of Group's Objectives and Tasks

Baseline Budget
Positions by Personnel Category • Nonpersonnel Expenses • Total

What are the group's objectives and tasks?

What is the baseline to be analyzed?

to existing accounts; marketing credit products to prospects; conducting third-party (such as brokers and lawyers) marketing; entertaining customers; and serving client relationships. Objectives, along with their corresponding tasks, are listed for each group until the responsibilities of every group member are represented.

The second step in understanding the group's objectives and tasks requires an identification of how each employee spends his or her time throughout the course of a year. Each employee is asked to divide time spent by the tasks defined for the group. The employees' time allocations, when multiplied by their respective salary levels, produce the total amount of personnel expense devoted to each task. A similar analysis is performed for each category of nonpersonnel expense.

When these data are compiled they produce a total cost for accomplishing each of the group's objectives. Using an automated database management system at this point is critical in order to carry out rigorous and varied analyses of, and comparisons between, departments and affiliates. These figures generate a number of surprises, when management realizes how much a particular item costs, or how many areas duplicate the same work throughout the organization. This analysis also helps in evaluating those areas that would benefit most from redesign, providing the basis for the next step: generating reengineering options.

Understanding Pricing

As reviewed in Chapter 3, the approach to pricing should be a pragmatic one that focuses explicitly on customer price elasticity at the transactional level. Properly executed, repricing can lead to a 15 to 20 percent increase in the bank's noninterest income, with negligible, if any, account runoff. The success of the effort, however, first requires that group leaders and working team members strengthen their understanding of the bank's existing pricing approach.

Contribution Analyzis

The starting point here is a close look at the overall economics of each of the bank's product and service offerings. An explicit cost/benefit analysis of each transaction's component parts is undertaken in order to thoroughly examine products and services at the subproduct level, involving the following analyses.

Unbundling

Pricing group leaders break down, or unbundle, the full range of products and services offered by each business area into the products' component parts. ATM services, for example, might be broken down into withdrawals, deposits, balance and account inquiries, fund transfers/payments, and "off-us" surcharges.

Revenue Baseline Development

Once products and services are unbundled, the revenues of each product or subproduct component can be determined. As a whole, ATM services, for example, might have produced total annual revenues of $500,000 while, separately, withdrawals may have amounted to $100,000 of that total; deposits, $20,000; balance and account inquiry, $100,000; fund transfers and payments, $80,000, and so on. A similar breakdown is developed for each product and service by business area, and serves as a foundation for the benefit side of the cost/benefit analysis.

Product Workflow Analysis

To understand the associated costs, group leaders map out the workflow and the major tasks of each product and service. (Figure 7.3 illustrates how one bank represented the workflow of its ATM services.) The diagrams depict the various cost components of each product and service. Group leaders confer with other employees in each business area in order to create a chart that most accurately describes each process.

Unit Cost Derivation and the Cost/Price Comparison

Once the product workflow diagram has been completed and the various cost components of each product have been identified, an analysis of the unit cost of each component can be undertaken. This involves comparing the unit cost of the product as a whole with the price per unit that is being charged. Using ATM services again as an example, one bank found that the total annual cost of the processing component was $2.9 million: $350,000 in personnel and $2.5 million in nonpersonnel costs. With 5 million transactions per annum, this translated into a processing cost on a per-unit basis of $0.57 consisting of $0.07 for personnel and $0.50 for nonpersonnel. For all components combined the cost per transaction amounted to $1.40

FIGURE 7.3

Workflow Chart—Automated Teller Machine

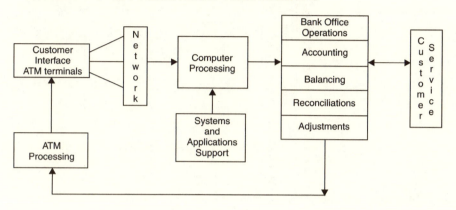

consisting of $0.40 in personnel cost and $1.00 in nonpersonnel. A comparison of the per-unit cost of $1.40 to the price per-unit of $0.25 which the bank currently charged on a bundled basis helped to set future ATM fees.

Customer Relationship Analysis

Part of understanding the cost of a bank's product and service offerings is identifying which customers contribute the most to cost and profit. Group leaders first estimate the revenues associated with specific customer segments and compare them to the transaction volumes and costs they generate by subproduct. The goal is to detect any imbalance between the level of tailored services provided to specific customer groups and the revenues obtained from them. Table 7.4 illustrates what one bank found in analyzing the economics of its corporate trust employee benefit plan customers. In short, the bank discovered that fewer than 8 percent of employee benefit plan customers, representing over 77 percent of the product's total assets, produced approximately 43 percent of total revenues and 8 percent of cost. At the same time, over 71 percent of its customers, representing just 7 percent of total assets, produced only 27 percent of total revenues and over 71 percent of total cost.

The analyses described above provide the framework for understanding pricing from a purely economic perspective. In addition to identi-

TABLE 7.4

Customer Relationship Analysis—Corporate Trust Service Employee Benefit Plans

No. of Customers	Amount (Thousands)	Total Assets	Average Assets/ Customer	Estimated Revenue Volume	Transaction Volumes by Subproduct			Estimated Costs by Subproduct		
					Record Keeping	Trans Activity	Administration	Record Keeping	Trans Activity	Administration
Managed:										
5 million	$ 9	188,581	20,953	$486	13	4,764	9	$9	$9	$25
3–5 million	8	28,290	3,536	146	5	4,235	8	4	8	22
1–3 million	36	57,426	1,595	305	34	19,057	26	23	37	100
under 1 million	175	65,545	375	506	152	92,639	175	104	180	485
Nonmanaged:										
5 million	$ 32	917,421	28,669	$758	4	16,940	32	$3	$33	$89
3–5 million	12	46,584	3,882	127	20	6,352	12	14	12	33
1–3 million	45	89,820	1,996	269	37	23,821	75	25	46	125
Under 1 million	180	37,467	208	291	80	95,286	180	55	185	499

fying the various revenue and cost components of the bank's existing product and service offerings, these analyses allow group leaders and working team members to assess the overall burden of tailoring transactions to customers' needs. In order to evaluate fully the prices being charged and investigate the opportunities for repricing, group leaders also determine the value the bank's customers place on services at the transactional level.

Value Analysis

To achieve a broader understanding of perceived customer value it is necessary to:

- Measure the level of importance customers attach to each product's main attributes.
- Compare the bank's ability to meet the needs of its customers with the ability of its main competitors.
- Examine each product in terms of the relationship between price and value.

This analysis in turn provides a foundation for assessing the "price band positioning" of each of the bank's products and services (i.e., the bank's price relative to competitors' for the respective value they provide) and allows group leaders to identify situations where the value of specific products exceeds the price charged. The following steps are taken to achieve this objective.

Identifying and Ranking Product Attributes

From a customer's perspective, attributes are defined as the specific needs fulfilled by each product. As an illustration, group leaders from one bank identified the main attributes of their ATM product as follows: convenience of location, 24-hour access, ease of use, security, types of transactions offered, printed transaction records, and reliability. Once the attributes of a product or service have been identified, the next step is to rank each attribute in terms of its relative importance to the bank's customers. Group leaders use their customer service experience, as well as the experiences of others in each business area, to develop this ranking.

In the ATM services example, group leaders in the consumer liability products area determined that their customers attached the greatest level of importance to the convenience of an ATM's location, followed by ability to access the machine on a 24-hour basis and the types of

TABLE 7.5

Ranking Subproduct Attributes—Consumer Liability
Products: ATM

Customer Needs	Importance to Customer
Convenience of location	30%
Access	20
Types of transactions	20
Ease of use	10
Security	5
Transaction records	5
Reliability	10
Index Total	100%

transaction offered. Progressively less important were the machine's ease of use, the reliability of the service it provided, the ability of the machines to produce printed transactions, and the level of security in place. (Table 7.5 provides additional information on the specific ranking of each attribute.) Upon establishing the importance of each product attribute to customers, group leaders rate the bank on its ability to meet the specific customer needs identified for a product or service on a scale of 1 to 10. (See Table 7.6.) To provide a basis for comparison, the same ranking is carried out for each of the bank's main competitors using available market and product information.

Determining Surplus Value Potential

The bank is prepared to compare its ability to meet customer needs with its competitors' abilities to do so, and to examine the relationship between the value that customers attach to products and the prices already being charged. Opportunities for repricing specific products, services, and transactions can be identified.

Such surplus value potential may be plotted graphically as the price the bank and its competitors charge for each product against the overall ability of each bank to meet the needs of its customers (i.e., its price band positioning). The relative location of each bank on the graph allows the group leader to identify situations where the perceived value of products and services is not in line with existing pricing, and may justify a price

TABLE 7.6

Rating the Bank on Its Ability to Meet Customer Needs–Consumer Liability Products: ATM

Rated on 1 to 10, 10 is best

Customer Needs:	Importance to Customer	Our Bank Service Level	Our Bank Index	Bank A Service Level	Bank A Index	Bank B Service Level	Bank B Index	Bank C Service Level	Bank C Index	Bank D Service Level	Bank D Index	Bank E Service Level	Bank E Index
Convenience of location	30%	7	210	8	240	3	90	4	120	8	240	8	240
Access	20	10	200	10	200	5	100	5	100	8	160	10	200
Ease of use	10	10	100	7	70	5	50	5	50	7	70	8	80
Security	5	5	25	7	35	0	0	0	0	2	10	7	35
Types of transactions	20	8	160	10	200	3	60	3	60	10	200	10	200
Transaction records	5	0	0	0	0	10	50	10	50	5	25	1	5
Reliability	10	7	70	7	70	5	50	6	60	10	100	7	70
Index Total	100%		765		815		400		440		805		830
Transaction price ($/unit)			0.25		0.20		0.20		0.30		0.35		0.50
Utility (weighted average svc index)			7.65		8.15		4.00		4.40		8.05		8.30
Utility/price (util/$)			31		41		20		15		23		17

FIGURE 7.4

Surplus Value Potential

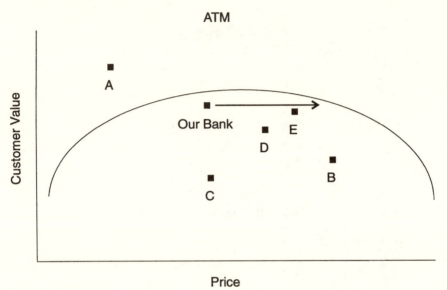

increase. Figure 7.4 illustrates how one bank's ATM product stacked up against its competitors. By completing the analysis described above the bank discovered that, relative to competitors, it was offering a more valuable product at a substantially lower price.

Market Analysis

Once we have examined the overall economics and the perceived customer value of each of the bank's product and service offerings, the final preparation necessary to begin repricing involves gathering information about the bank's existing market share, the success of its past pricing changes, its ability to control fee waivers, its commercial loan pricing potential, and its geographic market anomalies.

Historical Market Share

Looking at the bank's relative market share over time allows the pricing team to assess the level of success each business area has had with its product line. It also allows group leaders to observe evolving trends.

Gathering the information necessary to compare the market share of the bank with each of its main competitors over the preceding four years allows group leaders to evaluate the viability of repricing options.

Runoff Analysis

Banks are frequently concerned that a variety of price increases will have a severe impact on their current account, balance, and transaction levels. To allay this fear and help establish the available latitude for price increases, customer price sensitivity is analyzed. Group leaders first gather data showing the precise amount of each price change by product over the previous 18 to 24 months, competitor responses, and the number of accounts and net revenue lost as a result of the change, in order to identify any historical patterns of runoff. In most cases this serves to illustrate the rarity with which historical pricing changes impact revenues, typically less than 1 percent for price increases of even 20 percent.

Fee Waiver and Exemption Analysis

Group leaders gather data about the fee waivers granted to the bank's customers. These data detail the actual number of accounts waived and the dollar impact of those waivers by quarter over the previous 18 to 24 months. This information allows the group leaders and the working team to assess the regularity with which fee exemptions are made and to calculate their total economic impact. As an indication of how important this type of analysis can be, one bank discovered that these waivers and "escape clauses" amounted to over $4 million in lost revenue annually.

Pricing for Loan Default Risk

According to the simplest model, the price of a loan has four distinct components: funding costs; selling, general, and administrative expenses; a required return on capital; and a premium to compensate for default risk. There is compelling evidence that banks underprice for this last element, the riskiness of their loans.

This underpricing occurs when bankers implicitly consider their average default risk, without recognizing that short-term fluctuations away from the average may lead to the regulatory shutdown of the bank before the market has had a chance to correct itself. It is naive to assume that a bank may endure through the long run, because short-term excessive losses may jeopardize the bank's capital base. If capital erosion is significant, regulators may abruptly curtail the long run. Furthermore, bankers have traditionally priced the default components of their loans on the assumption that their loan portfolios are large and diversified.

Unfortunately, few regional (or community) banks have the geographic breadth to achieve an appropriately diversified portfolio. This further compounds the dangers of short-term loan loss fluctuations, because borrowers in related industries and common geographies are more likely to default in tandem, adversely skewing short-term losses. Banks must offset this short-term variability of loan losses through their loan pricing. Two banks, for example, may each have average loan losses of 1.5 percent. However, if bank A's annual losses range from 1.0 to 2.0 percent, whereas bank B's annual losses range from 0.0 to 3.0 percent, bank B clearly has a riskier customer base and must price its loans to compensate for this additional risk. The question is how to do so.

There are a number of ways to measure and price for default risk. The best makes use of the bank's own running history of loan losses, sorted by the bank's loan rating categories. To be specific, historical default data are gathered for each of the bank's loan rating categories (or other categories, based on available data, including the use of regional data from public sources). The methodology first examines carefully the pattern of loan defaults experienced by the bank in each of its loan rating categories. In most cases, the defaults will follow a normal distribution pattern over time.

The data are then used to generate a statistic that is directly added into the loan pricing formula as its risk term. The average and median alone are rejected because they do not incorporate short-term loan loss fluctuations. The statistic combines instead the mean with one-half of the standard deviation. Regression studies performed by Diversified Corporate Loans, Inc. have demonstrated that this measure of risk is the best predictor of market returns on a bank's stock. By adding half of the standard deviation to the mean, an additional 19 percent of the likely loan charge-offs will be captured. An example is provided in Figure 7.5.

As plotted, the average default rate for the entire portfolio is 2.0 percent and the standard deviation is 3.0 percentage points. In this case, therefore, the risk pricing term is 3.5 percent and the 150 basis points which are added to the mean substantially correct for the variability in the bank's charge-offs for its risk-rated three loans.

Pricing for Geographic Differentiation
In order to capitalize on geographic differentials in loan and deposit pricing, two analyses should be carried out.

FIGURE 7.5

Pricing for Loan Default Risk
Default Rates—Loans in Risk Rating 3

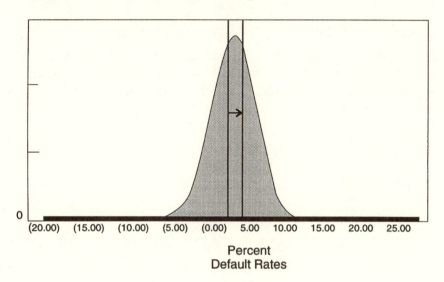

Percent
Default Rates

Intrastate Position   The bank's existing pricing for each product and transaction should be compared with competitors in each local market (town, region and so on). This comparison will at least indicate where the bank already stands on the competitive price band and indicate opportunities to move closer to a price leader. Also, where legally permissible, differential pricing by competitors across local markets may suggest potential to price at different levels for the same product/transaction in distinct local markets. Take New York State, for example. There is often a 30 to 50-basis-point differential in the rate paid on six-month certificates of deposit between Manhattan and, for example, Rochester. Yet, many banks have set statewide rates.

Interstate Position   Comparable to the second situation above, it is surprising how many multistate holding companies charge the same price for products and transactions across states. The relative price elasticity of customers and the competitive dynamics of each state may, however, be widely different. Recognizing these contrasts can be the source of significant differential pricing opportunities. Moreover, within each state, the local market distinctions discussed above can then be capitalized upon.

IN CONCLUSION

The preparatory steps of reengineering are tough work. They involve painstaking, detailed analysis of the whole bank's costs and pricing approach. But they only set the stage for the most exciting part of bank reengineering: idea development, which is outlined next.

CHAPTER 8

A Systematic Approach to Bank Reengineering– Idea Development

GENERATING REENGINEERING OPTIONS

The most stimulating and creative phase of reengineering is generating the options that will form the basis for organizational and business redesign: no stone is left unturned in the effort to find and analyze ideas for change (Table 8.1). Every member of the organization is involved in generating ideas, improving them, and determining their impact on earnings.

The goal is to generate reengineering options that make up 40 percent of the groups' baseline budgets. The 40 percent figure is a stretch target; it is not a program for 40 percent earnings improvement. Rather, the target is established to help everyone look everywhere for ideas, drawing on creative thinking for radical approaches to changing process costs radically or increasing revenues. It forces the basic assumptions underlying an objective to be questioned, rather than the mere examination of whether tasks are being performed efficiently. Generating reengineering options has four components:

- ◆ Creation of an idea database.
- ◆ Refinement of ideas.
- ◆ Evaluation of ideas.
- ◆ Upgrading of ideas.

Figure 8.1 provides an illustration of this process. The approach is iterative, requiring each group leader to generate, analyze, and refine ideas built around radical, comprehensive, redesign themes set "top-down" and

TABLE 8.1

The Six-Step Approach to Reengineering

Step	Major Components	Chapter
Preparing for change	Psychological preparation Cost preparation Repricing preparation	7
Understanding current processes	Understanding processes and costs	7
Understanding current pricing	Contrubition analysis Product workflow analysis Unit cost derivation Customer relationship analysis Value analysis	7
Generating reengineering options	**Top-down approaches for process cost design** **Top-down approaches for repricing** **Bottom-up approach**	**8**
Refining options	**Evaluation of the options** **Upgrading ideas**	**8**
Charting the new bank's course	Planning the future Tracking achievement Avoiding execution pitfalls Re-commitment of the new bank	9

their associated earnings impact. Each idea is submitted for evaluation to all other areas in the organization which are affected by it to address the complex interdependencies of change across the bank. Last, based upon this feedback, the bank improves or upgrades the idea to maximize savings or benefits and to minimize the level of associated risk. The new idea is then resubmitted to the idea evaluators in a circular process.

Not every idea within the idea portfolio will be implemented. Some ideas will be deemed too risky in the sense that they may, for example, impair credit quality, jeopardize customer service, reduce marketing efforts, or damage the bank's reputation in the community. Table 8.2 shows the range of risk profiles that may emerge.

The challenge for the group leaders and the working team is clearly to generate the best ideas for their idea portfolios. In the following phase of the process, the management committee will make decisions on whether to approve or reject the ideas for implementation. The goal of generating

FIGURE 8.1

Generating Reengineering Options

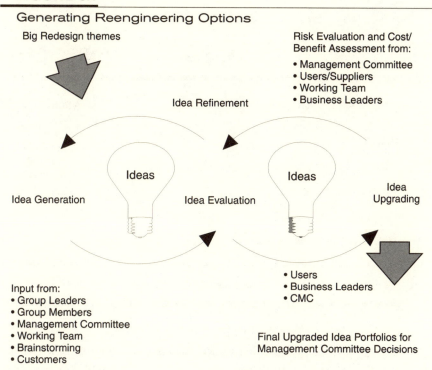

Big Redesign themes

Risk Evaluation and Cost/
Benefit Assessment from:

• Management Committee
• Users/Suppliers
• Working Team
• Business Leaders

Idea Refinement

Ideas   Ideas

Idea Generation   Idea Evaluation   Idea Upgrading

Input from:
• Group Leaders
• Group Members
• Management Committee
• Working Team
• Brainstorming
• Customers

• Users
• Business Leaders
• CMC

Final Upgraded Idea Portfolios for
Management Committee Decisions

TABLE 8–2

Risk Profiles of Idea Portfolios Vary by Group

Group	A	B	C	D	E	
Idea base	**51%**	**47%**	**43%**	**45%**	**42%**	
Low risk	41	13	18	36	42	Likely to be implemented
Medium risk	7	14	18	4	0	Most will be implemented
High risk	3	20	7	5	0	Many will be implemented

reengineering options, however, is to produce a portfolio with a large number of ideas, low-risk ratings and high earnings impact.

The group leaders are responsible for assembling the database of ideas. Yet, they do not work in a vacuum. They collaborate with each other,

FIGURE 8.2

Idea flow-Process Cost Groups

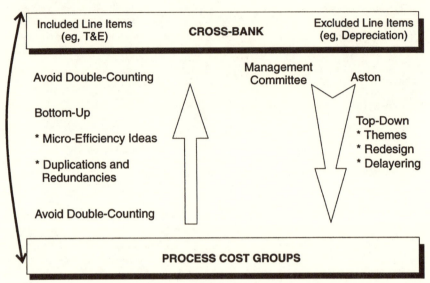

with other employees, and with senior managers, drawing upon all the resources and staff of the organization. The approach is both top-down and bottom-up. In other words, the management committee and business leaders will suggest themes for the group leaders to evaluate on the process and repricing fronts, and ideas will flow upward to the group leaders from employees who create ways to improve their day-to-day tasks as a result. Figure 8.2 illustrates this two-way flow of ideas for change, and also illustrates the fact that several of the working team members simultaneously develop cross-bank ideas by challenging the policies that underlie each line item of expense in the bank (a horizontal review of many of the same processes, practices, and procedures that the group leaders are considering vertically).

Top-Down Approaches for Process Cost Redesign

In addition to those ideas generated by the individual groups, a key part of reengineering requires the management committee to identify structural redesign ideas for each area on the process side to evaluate. These areas can be broadly classified as the branch network, retail credit, wholesale, trust, systems and operations, administration, and consolidation. In the following sections, some redesign ideas (or themes) will be outlined.

Branch Network

The first step in determining a redesign theme is to identify the underlying process characteristics of the area. The characteristics of the branch system can be broadly defined to include processing, administration, sales, and customer service. In most organizations, a full two-thirds of branch personnel's time is devoted to processing and administration, objectives that are not customer-focused. In addition, customer service consists of two components: in-person service and telephone service. The telephone portion of customer service detracts from the time spent with the customers who have taken the time to come to the branch and can be cross-sold the bank's products in person.

One of the key themes for retail branches is, therefore, to provide more of a customer orientation by removing their back-office processing and administrative activities. Several redesign ideas accompany this theme: centralizing customer service, redesigning deposit operations, and regionalizing transaction processing.

Centralizing customer service involves several components: using an automated response system to handle simple inquiries, such as balances, rates, and check clearing; using highly trained customer service representatives situated in a separate customer service center to handle complex requests, complaints, and the coordination of internal problem-solving efforts; and, on a simple yet extremely effective level, publishing only the customer service center's telephone number rather than the branches'. For each theme that is developed, a rigorous costing methodology has to be devised that establishes benchmarks for performance for the reengineered process. Without such an approach the savings impact may not be achieved.

Through experience and research, Aston Associates has developed benchmarks for every area of a bank (although providing an in-depth discussion of each of these methodologies would need another book). Table 8.3 illustrates such a methodology for the customer service option.

As can be seen from Table 8.3, the first part of the methodology involves gathering information on the number of calls received by the branches. These calls are divided into four categories: inquiry; problem solving; transaction issues; and product information. Each group leader

TABLE 8.3

Centralize Customer Service: Data Summary

Group 1	Branch	Branch	Branch	Branch	Branch	Average
Average daily number of calls by type per branch						
Inquiry	57	50	63	55	60	57
Product information	26	30	24	19	31	26
Problem solving	36	28	42	39	35	36
Transaction issues	11	9	13	11	11	11
Average daily calls per branch	130	117	142	124	137	130
Group 2						
Average daily number of calls by type per branch						
Inquiry	59	55	58	56	57	57
Product information	28	26	25	24	27	26
Problem solving	35	37	35	37	36	36
Transaction issues	10	11	11	11	12	11
Average daily calls per branch	132	129	129	128	132	130
Group 3						
Average daily number of calls by type per branch						
Inquiry	20	30	25	24	26	25
Product information	59	57	62	63	59	60
Problem solving	2	8	4	5	6	5
Transaction issues	3	5	6	4	7	5
Average daily calls per branch	84	100	97	96	98	95
Group 4						
Average daily number of calls by type per branch						
Inquiry	40	29	32	38	36	35
Product information	18	22	20	19	21	20
Problem solving	29	32	31	29	29	30
Transaction issues	16	24	19	20	21	20
Average daily calls per branch	103	107	102	106	107	105
Group 5						
Average daily number of calls by type per branch						
Inquiry	21	16	18	23	22	20
Product information	12	8	7	9	4	10
Problem solving	26	15	18	20	21	20
Transaction issues	7	8	14	10	11	10
Average daily calls per branch	66	47	57	62	68	60

TABLE 8.3

Centralize Customer Service: Analysis

Allocation Basis	Assumptions	Group 1	Group 2	Group 3	Group 4	Group 5	Total
Number of branches		49	33	49	36	30	197
Average Daily Number of Calls by Type per Branch							
Inquiry		57	57	25	35	20	194
Product information		26	26	60	20	10	142
Problem solving		36	36	5	30	20	127
Transaction issues		11	11	5	20	10	57
Average daily calls per branch		130	130	95	105	60	520
Average Daily Number of Calls by Type per Group							
Inquiry		2,793	1,881	1,225	1,260	600	7,759
Product information		1,274	858	2,940	720	300	6,092
Problem solving		1,764	1,188	245	1,080	600	4,877
Transaction issues		539	363	245	720	300	2,167
Average daily calls per group	6,370	4,290	4,655	3,780	1,800	20,895	
Average Daily Number of Calls to Customer Service							
Inquiry	Factor = 95%	2,653	1,787	1,164	1,197	570	7,371
Product information	Factor = 100	1,274	858	2,940	720	300	6,092
Problem solving	Factor = 80	1,411	950	196	864	480	3,902
Transaction issues	Factor = 85	458	309	208	612	255	1,842
Average daily customer service calls		5,797	3,904	4,508	3,393	1,605	19,207
Average Daily Minutes Saved per Group							
Inquiry	Minutes = 3.0	7,960	5,361	3,491	3,591	1,710	22,113
Product information	Minutes = 4.0	5,096	3,432	11,760	2,880	1,200	24,368
Problem solving	Minutes = 7.0	9,878	6,653	1,372	6,048	3,360	27,311
Transaction issues	Minutes = 4.0	1,833	1,234	833	2,448	1,020	7,368
Average daily minutes saved per group		24,767	16,680	17,456	14,967	7,290	81,160
Average Daily Hours/FTEs Saved							
Total hours saved per group		413	278	291	249	122	1,353
Total hours saved per branch		8	8	6	7	4	34
Total FTEs saved per branch	Hr/FTE = 8.0	1.05	1.05	0.74	0.87	0.51	4.22
Total FTEs saved per group		51.60	34.75	36.37	31.18	15.19	169.08

TABLE 8.3

Centralize Customer Service: Buildups

Average Daily Customer Service Ccalls	Assumptions	Group 1	Group 2	Group 3	Group 4	Group 5	Total
Inquiry		2,653	1,787	1,164	1,197	570	7,371
Product information		1,274	858	2,940	720	300	6,092
Problem solving		1,411	950	196	864	480	3,902
Transaction issues		458	309	208	612	255	1,842
Total customer service calls		5,797	3,904	4,508	3,393	1,605	19,207
Average Daily Automated Calls							
Inquiry	Factor = 60%	1,592	1,072	698	718	342	4,423
Product information	Factor = 60	764	515	1,764	432	180	3,655
Problem solving	Factor = 30	423	285	59	259	144	1,170
Transaction issues	Factor = 25	115	77	52	153	64	460
Total Automated Calls		2,894	1,949	2,573	1,562	730	9,709
Percent of Total Calls		49.9%	49.9%	57.1%	46.0%	45.5%	50.5%
Average Daily Agent Calls							
Inquiry	Factor = 40%	1,061	715	466	479	228	2,948
Product information	Factor = 40	510	343	1,176	288	120	2,437
Problem solving	Factor = 70	988	665	137	605	336	2,731
Transaction issues	Factor = 75	344	231	156	459	191	1,381
Total agent calls		2,902	1,955	1,935	1,831	875	9,498
percent of total calls		50.1%	50.1%	42.9%	54.0%	54.5%	49.5%
Average Daily Customer Service Agent Minutes							
Inquiry	Minutes = 1.5	1,592	1,072	698	718	342	4,423
Product information	Minutes = 2.0	1,019	686	2,352	576	240	4,874
Problem solving	Minutes = 3.5	3,457	2,328	480	2,117	1,176	9,559
Transaction issues	Minutes = 2.0	687	463	312	918	383	2,763
Total agent minutes		6,756	4,550	3,843	4,329	2,141	21,618
Customer Service Agents Required							
Number of agents (MNE)	minutes/agent = 360	18.8	12.6	10.7	12.0	5.9	60.1

surveys several branches to estimate the number of each type of call received and the amount of time branch personnel spend responding to each.

The percentage of each type of call which could potentially be handled by a centralized customer service unit is evaluated. This percentage should represent the vast majority of calls as, usually, only a few specialized inquiries need to be sent back to the branches for resolution. In the example, 95 percent of inquiries, 100 percent of product information, 80 percent of problem solving, and 84 percent of transaction issues are capable of being handled at the customer service center.

This results in a savings per branch of 0.50 to 1.00 full-time equivalent employees. In a bank with almost 200 branches, this translates to a gross FTE reduction of almost 170 people.

The customer service unit must, however, be sufficiently staffed to handle these calls. The use of benchmarks at this point is critical to estimate the needs of the buildup organization. The service center calculates the percentage of calls forwarded to the center that could be handled by the automated response system. (The percentages set forth in the example are typical of the results achieved with an automated system.) Any remaining calls are referred to customer service agents.

As can be seen in the example, customer service agents spend substantially less time per call answering customers' questions. This is because they have on-line terminals ready to access all the required customer account or product information.

These benchmarks produce an estimated 60 customer service agents required to staff the central service unit, which, in turn, produces a net personnel savings of 110 employees. There are, of course, nonpersonnel costs involved that have not been illustrated here, which must be taken into account when calculating the net savings of the idea.

Centralizing customer service is an excellent example of how process redesign can result in better service quality, for both in-branch and telephone customers, while producing significant savings for the bank. (Although costing methodologies will not be illustrated for the remaining redesign ideas, such methodologies are integral to successfully executing a top-down approach.)

Automating the platform can also enhance the quality of customer service delivered in the branch network. Automation systems must be carefully analyzed, however, to prevent overkill. One simple example of overautomation is the use of personal computer software that requires a mouse; branch personnel who use them tend to spend most of their time looking at the computer screen, rather than at the customer.

When used correctly, however, platform automation can greatly improve interaction with customers. A streamlined automation system will require information only once as opposed to requiring the customer to provide the same information repeatedly. It can also broaden the skill mix of customer service representatives (CSRs) by providing cross-selling tools and linkages with the central customer information files.

Redesigning deposit operations (payment processing, tax and regulatory services, reporting requirements, and reconciliations) is a prime area for reengineering. Many of these activities are typically performed in the branches, and then the relevant paperwork is forwarded to the deposit operations area, where its processing is completed. The advantage of centralizing all these tasks within the operations area is that the operations specialists are generally more efficient because they are not constantly interrupted by customers. In the branches, the tellers and CSRs can devote more of their time to interacting with and cross-selling to customers.

Regionalizing transaction processing affects nonwindow deposits such as night safe, ATM, and postal deposits. Branch personnel can be freed to devote more time to customers by establishing regional centers for processing these deposits, which can be collected by armored car runs. The regional centers debit or credit customers' accounts upon receipt, process the deposits during the evening or night shift, and make any required adjustments the following day.

Additional themes related to the branch network focus not only on how service is delivered but on where it is delivered. A hub-and-spoke configuration provides customers with the services they most desire in the most convenient locations. Although an often-discussed concept, the crux of this distribution system is execution, not design. It contrasts with the typical branch structure, which provides only full-service outlets, by designing tailored outlets for differentiated levels of service.

The hub-and-spoke structure is a broad concept. The specific design parameters for full-service and limited-service branches must be tailored to each individual bank. A 400-branch bank adopted this approach to retail delivery. The bank initially established five criteria for limited-service branches:

+ Average total deposits less than $15 million.

- Average total loans less than $2 million.
- Total monthly transactions less than $10 million.
- Locations in a market area characterized as stable with slow to moderate growth potential.
- Operations exceeding five years.

Employing these criteria, management was able to designate one-third of the branches as limited-service outlets. This was a very conservative designation, which was developed once the bank gained experience with the hub-and-spoke structure.

The bank defined the limited-service (or spokes) branches as strictly transaction facilities, without lending authority. Their employees were thus assigned only limited responsibility for business development or relationship management. The spokes could be run by assistant managers, therefore, often as management entry-level positions for retail associates (recent graduates of the bank's retail training program).

The hub branches, on the other hand, were responsible for sales and servicing for all retail deposits, loan and third-party products, and services to consumers and small businesses in the bank's markets. The hub branches were staffed with retail credit officers who supported the surrounding spokes branches and managed client relationships and business development efforts in the area.

The net result of changing the branch delivery system and the corresponding shifts in branch and regional management was cost savings of $600,000 annually. Additional savings were available as the bank became more comfortable with the structure and more branches were designated as limited service.

A network of full-service and limited-service branches allows the organization to staff outlets more appropriately. In the hub branch, regional management layers can be removed if the span of control is increased. In the spokes branches, administrative layers can be removed. Because the spoke branch is transaction-oriented, rather than loan-oriented, the branch manager does not have to be credit-trained and the role can be filled by lower-paid personnel. A primary benefit of this type of structure is that it removes the layers between branch managers and their customers, thus increasing the responsiveness of each location to the market that it serves.

The central theme, therefore, of the branch network process changes is to place the branch staff closer to the customer. While generating cost savings, each of these themes also improves the service quality and selling opportunities available at appropriate branches.

Retail Credit

Retail credit is characterized by the same administrative burdens as in the branches. There are often processing inefficiencies that result from a delivery system whose outlets are not sufficiently tailored to their markets, with an overly complex product line and a cumbersome matrix structure for credit approval.

Tailoring delivery points to local markets is similar to the hub-and-spoke concept in the branch network. Private banking, small business, installment, and consumer loans and mortgages are not demanded by customers at every branch location. Creating specialized loan centers in the areas of greatest demand makes the best use of the bank's staff, while providing convenience and expertise for its customers. Establishing appropriate staffing of these centers is an important part of the benchmarking process.

Multiple product variations are typical in many retail credit product lines. These variations often have resulted from prior acquisitions. In other instances, when new product lines were developed to enhance a previous product, the old product was never discontinued. Too many complex products can create customer confusion, impair the sales effort of retail credit personnel and delay turnaround time. As a result, the bank is forced to charge higher rates in order to cover the high cost of these complex product offerings.

Most retail customers do not require a wide loan product choice. A simple installment loan and a line of credit will generally serve their needs. Simplifying the product line reduces confusion and streamlines processing, enabling one-day loan approvals to be offered. The bank's profitability is enhanced through lower costs and greater market share, as rate reductions thereby become possible.

Credit automation benefits are one result of a simplified product line delivered through an on-line application system to branches, automobile dealers and mortgage brokers. This application system is networked to a loan center, where the applications are automatically prescreened. The system then scores the loan, based on parameters determined by the bank and, if approved, produces the required documentation. The benefits of this approach are improved turnaround times, a consistent application of the bank's credit standards, and a streamlined information request from the customer.

Automating the retail credit process saved $500,000 at one U.S. bank in the Northeast. The system implemented was comprehensive but simple.

It allowed for centralized or decentralized application processing and decision-making capabilities; loan document preparation; pre-screening of applications; credit scoring with multiple "scorecard" interface capabilities; and automated production of customer letters, transaction records, and tract reporting for legislative purposes.

In addition to the cost savings achieved, the retail scoring system produced other significant benefits. Loan decisions were made in minutes rather than days. This increased market penetration, both with consumers directly and with automobile dealers. In addition, underwriting standards were consistently applied and enforced, leading to improved credit quality. Moreover, the new system also added to the productivity of the branch and the processing staff. Many time-consuming, repetitive, manual processes were eliminated. This allowed branch staff to be more responsive to customers and reduced the number of errors in all stages of processing. This type of investment, therefore, produced cost savings, customer service benefits, and employee morale improvements.

An often overlooked area for credit automation is in the collections department which can allow the bank to increase the account load per collector and, more importantly, provide a valuable reporting mechanism to management. Figure 8.3 illustrates the limited number of banks that already had selected collection software features.

Parallel sets of processes often exist for each type of retail loan with each product line having its own manager, system, and process. By combining the process aspects by function, rather than by product line, the bank can fully integrate its customer information files and provide a more effective, streamlined processing system.

This can be particularly important to a customer having several loan relationships with a bank. If such a customer has a mortgage and wants an automobile loan, for example, the customer traditionally has to initiate the process as though he or she is unknown by the bank. By integrating the process across product lines, the bank can better assess the creditworthiness of the customer and streamline its processing and servicing, while providing a higher level of service.

The bank described above took advantage of its credit scoring system by implementing it across the various retail credit products. Although the parameters were set differently for each type of loan, the system allowed for a single underwriting and documentation process. The bank also created a central documentation unit to store and access documents for installment lending, leasing, and mortgages. Last, the bank centralized the collection

FIGURE 8.3

Automated Collections Tools

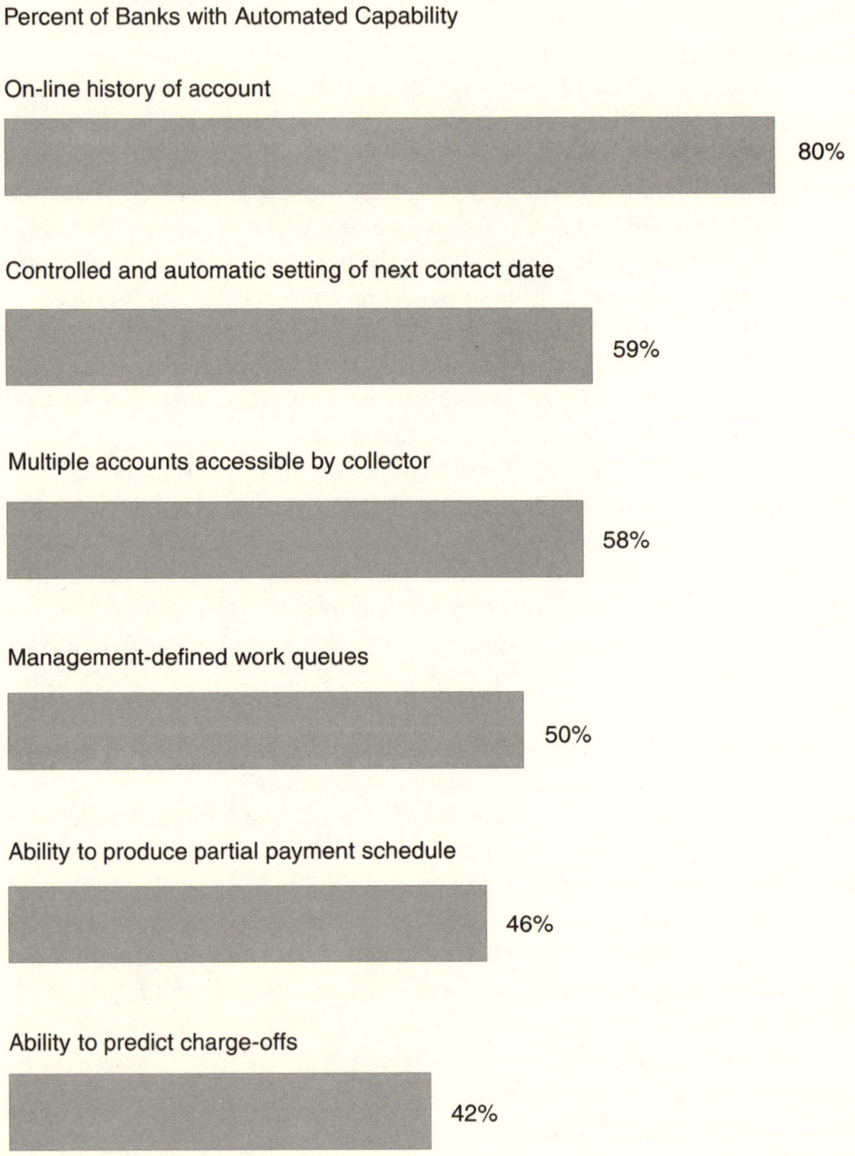

Percent of Banks with Automated Capability

On-line history of account

80%

Controlled and automatic setting of next contact date

59%

Multiple accounts accessible by collector

58%

Management-defined work queues

50%

Ability to produce partial payment schedule

46%

Ability to predict charge-offs

42%

Source: CyberResources Corp.

function for all areas of retail credit. Combining similar, parallel processes into a single, common process resulted in a cost savings of more than $2 million.

Wholesale

The typical wholesale distribution system is not tailored to differing market or customer needs. Marketing resources are generally not deployed properly on the highest priority accounts, and marketing officers are burdened by excessive administrative tasks. Administrative assistants traditionally support the account officers but do not interact with the customer. Account officers have clerical, lending analysis, structuring, and underwriting responsibilities. Moreover, a common product set, with a common loan approval process and standard documentation requirements, is marketed to all customers regardless of loan size.

The themes related to wholesale involve redesigning the marketing approach (and, therefore, the role of account officers) and tailoring the product mix by customer segment.

Redesign Wholesale Distribution
In a redesigned approach, administrative assistants perform the clerical support, lending analysis (spreadsheet) functions and much of the day-to-day problem solving for customers, freeing account officers for more advanced responsibilities.

In addition, a distinction is made between marketing and credit functions. This creates two classes of account officers: the business development officer and the underwriting officer. The business development officer acts as the relationship manager, responsible for responding to all the corporate customer's needs. He or she also has the responsibility for developing new business. The underwriting (or credit) officer is responsible for executing specific transactions.

This type of division of responsibilities is similar to the traditional approach to asset-based lending. It is successful because the nonselling responsibilities are removed from the relationship manager, who can devote more time to serving existing customers and calling on prospects. The credit officer develops specialized analytical skills that contribute to better structured loans and higher credit quality.

Simplify the Product Mix
The redesigned system may call for the creation of a small business lending unit offering standard generic products supported by an automated credit approval process with standard

documentation. For larger corporate customers a multiple product set continues to offer tailored products and documentation to serve their more sophisticated borrowing, trade, and cash management needs.

The new approach thus focuses on matching the cost of the delivery system with the value placed upon the products and service levels by differing types of customer. A low-cost delivery system for the small business customer enhances the bank's competitiveness in this profitable market and improves the response time for the customer. Additional time can then be spent on serving larger customers' more complex requirements.

Consider the wholesale business of a commercial bank in the Northeast of the United States. Although its officers were known as quality service providers to their existing clients, the bank was concerned about its ability to generate new business with existing staff. In examining the responsibilities of the relationship managers, it became clear that they were overburdened with administrative tasks. In addition, smaller clients (in terms of loan size) were receiving as much attention as the largest clients, if not more. In reengineering its organization, the department shifted many client management responsibilities to the administrative staff, and removed many smaller loan and deposit-only customers from the account officers. By leveraging support personnel and pruning unprofitable accounts from the wholesale distribution system, relationship managers were able to increase their account loads by more than 20 percent. The department also set origination goals for its officers that were substantially above the level of origination previously generated. Last, as account loads were rationalized, the managerial span of control over employees and geographies was streamlined to accommodate the new approach.

This business approach and organizational redesign resulted in a much more customer-oriented department with greatly enhanced business development capabilities. The wholesale department was able to generate cost savings of $4.4 million, or 19 percent of its total cost base.

Trust

An astounding aspect of the trust business is the sheer number of accounts that are not profitable for the bank. Fewer than 20 percent of trust customers provide more than 80 percent of the profits for most banks. The primary reason for this is that the distribution system does not distinguish between low-end and high-end customers. There is little or no differentiation in the product offering and level of marketing effort deployed across profitable and unprofitable accounts. Raising prices for low-end customers is often not a solution, as this raises the cost to customers above the value they place upon the service. The central themes in redesigning the trust business are tiering service levels and tiering product mix.

Marketing Approach   In a traditional institution a corporate treasurer is called upon by officers from many parts of the bank: by private banking and personal trust officers for personal financial needs; and by wholesale, cash management, corporate trust, and employee benefits salespeople for the corporation's financial needs. It is not surprising that the corporate treasurer does not know which officer to call upon with a problem. This is also a very expensive system for any bank to maintain.

Consolidating these calling responsibilities provides a more streamlined method of contact between the bank and the corporate treasurer, and reduces the cost of delivering high-quality service. The redesign of trust, therefore, involves coordinating the origination responsibilities of all areas of the bank. For a customer's personal financial needs, there is a single personal finance officer who offers private banking and personal trust products. On the corporate side, a corporate finance officer markets wholesale loans, trade finance, cash management services, corporate trust products, and employee benefit products.

The personal and corporate finance officers are supported by a network of product and service specialists who are called upon, as needed, to execute and close transactions. The customer, therefore, has only one person in each capacity to service all of his or her financial needs; the customer no longer needs to become an expert concerning the product divisions of the bank.

Product Mix   The traditional trust product mix is very similar to the traditional wholesale mix. Tailored products are offered to both high- and low-end customers, without regard to the value the customer places upon this level of service. In aligning cost and value, a standard set of products is offered to the low-end accounts that makes these services profitable for the bank and price-competitive for the customer. High-value tailored products continue to be offered to high-end account holders, who are willing and able to pay for the additional cost of specialized services. As the bank's trust products become more profitable for both types of customers, greater market share can be achieved because prices can be varied by account type.

Tiering the customer service levels among accounts, for example, yielded dramatic results for one Midwestern bank. Prior to its reengineering, the personal trust department serviced its accounts with a team consisting of a trust officer, an administrator, and a secretary. The teams were assigned accounts randomly rather than by account size or fee value. The bank also offered an undifferentiated array of sophisticated trust products, although these products were frequently further tailored to customers' requests.

This misallocation of resources was evident when accounts were analyzed for profitability. It was found that almost 40 percent of the living trusts (a product which accounted for 65 percent of personal trust's revenues) were unprofitable. Nine percent of the trust group's accounts generated 40 percent of the fees. In addition, over half of the accounts generated less than $2,750 each in annual revenues.

After a careful examination of its customers, the personal trust group developed a tiered service structure. Tier I servicing was designed for the bank's most valued family accounts, providing the highest service level, individually managed portfolios, and the most tailored product mix. Tier II servicing was structured for the majority of the customer base with standard model portfolios but individual customer consultations. Officers of tier II accounts were assigned a substantially larger account base than officers of tier I accounts. Last, tier III servicing was designed to be provided by a customer service area, rather than by individual trust officers. This type of servicing was made possible because the tier III product choices were limited to common trust funds. These changes, after the automation cost required to implement the approach, resulted in a decrease of almost 25 percent in the size of the personal trust staff and generated savings of approximately $1.2 million.

Systems and Operations

The intimidating technical aspects of systems and operations can often deter basic redesign. Operations areas are nevertheless often burdened with inefficient workflows, insufficient automation, and redundant controls. Unnecessary workflows often result from automating the manual steps of a process rather than examining whether the work should (or could) flow differently in an automated environment. Other inefficiencies result from maintaining parallel manual and automated processing beyond the testing period of a new system. The themes to explore follow.

Systematically Examine the Flow of Work and Redesign the Overall Process   Redesign is not a matter of improving the efficiency of the existing process. Rather, it involves resequencing

activities to eliminate unnecessary steps and the need for repetitive checks and controls. It may also require automating repetitive processes or eliminating a manual function that already is automated. To accomplish this type of redesign, the group leader needs to step back from the detail and examine what is appropriate. The manager can then rely upon more junior level employees to implement the more technical aspects of the redesign.

Challenge the Basic Assumption of the Operation

Is the operation needed? Why? What customer or user need does it fulfil? Is there a better way to meet this need? A prime example of challenging the basic assumption underlying an operation relates to returning checks with a customer's statement. The need met by returning the checks is that it creates a (bulky) record for problem resolution. A better way to meet this need, and create expense savings for the bank, is to store the customer's canceled checks and provide access on demand only to those needed for specific customer problem resolution.

Require a Cost/Benefit Justification for New
Systems and Enhancements
Systems projects tend to become bigger, more elaborate, and more expensive as they progress. Continually changing user requirements, insufficient costing, and a lack of clarity on the cost and value of "frills" are only some of the factors that contribute to this tendency. Once developed, systems projects often do not achieve their projected savings because their implementation stretches beyond the projected time frame and the tracking of cost reductions is often inadequate.

The two basic questions to ask with regard to a systems project are: "Do we need it?" and "Can we afford it?" Each project, whether it involves a new system or an enhancement or modification of an existing system, should require a strict cost/benefit justification. In addition, prior to development, overly complex modules, which require excessive maintenance, should be evaluated for outsourcing, rather than in-house development. The Star Banc case study provides a detailed example of the reengineering of systems and operations for Star Banc, Cincinnati, which saved 20 percent of total cost.

Administration

The relevant questions to ask when examining administrative processes are: "What do the administrative areas do?" and "Are their outputs used effectively by the bank's internal client areas?" As administrative staffs increase, more and more levels of analysis are performed. At some point, however, this results in information overload, as the people who receive the data cannot absorb all the information presented.

Reengineering themes for administrative departments focus on the level of detail in each function. Examples include: streamlining the budgeting and planning process, standardising benefit programs, establishing minimum and maximum compliance levels, and reducing the scope and frequency of audits. The redesign of administration acknowledges that each area serves a very valuable function but also examines demand from the users' perspective to ensure that all the information produced is needed.

One bank, for example, was able to save over $150,000 by reducing the amount of research and information generated by the human resources system alone, as it became apparent that much of these data were never used. The bank was able to save another $27,000 by consolidating three different employee newsletters into a single, comprehensive publication. This not only saved money but also ensured that employees received a consistent message from the bank.

Consolidation

Parallel organizational structures within the bank should be examined for consolidation opportunities. As discussed in Chapters 2 to 4, past acquisitions have led to many acquired institutions not being sufficiently integrated into the acquiring organization. This has often resulted in the proliferation of duplicative human resources, accounting, legal, compliance, and other administrative departments. Multiple data and processing centers have been created with little geographic or functional rationale.

Consolidation of these parallel structures can result in tremendous savings for the organization, but usually requires the highest level of support from senior management to ensure seamless and efficient execution. In my experience, as much as one-third of total reengineering savings can be achieved from truly consolidating affiliates (without undermining local identity as far as customers are concerned).

Consider one bank that had acquired 12 banks over the preceding five years. Each bank, in order to preserve its local identity, had been left alone since its acquisition and had its own administrative and operations support. As the affiliate banks examined opportunities for reengineering it became apparent that these back-office functions contributed little to the banks' community presence and often created customer confusion because of a proliferation of nonstandard products and services.

The affiliates considered consolidating the administrative areas of training, accounting and finance, legal, human resources, marketing, and purchasing and supply. It was determined that consolidating the purchasing and supply function across the 12 geographically dispersed affiliates would not create cost savings and might impair local business relationships. However, consolidation of the other functions was determined to have little or no impact on the community and saved $2.2 million, net of all implementation costs. Although many of these savings resulted from a reduction of employees, a significant amount was saved in nonpersonnel expense, as economies of scale reduced marketing, legal, and systems costs.

The operations areas were evaluated for consolidation efficiencies as well. Three of the affiliates had deposit services areas which would sort, count, and batch deposit tickets for transport to the flagship bank's deposit operations department. When received at the central operations center the center's staff would unbundle, resort, recount, and rebatch the tickets. When the operations areas were combined and the redundant activities eliminated, the net cost savings amounted to $600,000.

Cross-Bank Cost Analysis

In addition to the identification and evaluation of process redesign ideas by business areas discussed above, dedicated working team members also examine cost issues that affect the organization corporatewide. This is a horizontal look at budget line item expenses that occur in parallel with the vertical reengineering approach in the groups. Cross-bank costs are principally nonpersonnel in nature and are often overlooked because of a tendency to underestimate the savings potential of such a review. In fact, a substantial amount of cost can be eliminated from an organization in this way. One bank saved more than $2.3 million; another about $4.0 million.

Cross-bank expense items include armored car and messenger services; travel and entertainment; dues and subscriptions; seminars, training, and recruitment expenses; postage and printing; marketing and public affairs; contributions; directors' fees; equipment repairs and maintenance; and software purchases. The relevant questions to ask when examining these issues are:

- What policies do we already have with respect to these expenditures?
- How recently have the policies been reviewed and updated?
- How can the company's use of outside vendors be consolidated to make relationships more cost-effective?

- ◆ Can outsourced services be brought in-house at a lower cost, or vice versa?
- ◆ Can services already being provided in-house be centralized to eliminate the duplication of cost at subsidiaries?

To illustrate how this analysis can translate into significant savings, the following examples show the savings produced for a West Coast bank:

- ◆ Savings of more than 20 percent were achieved by requiring upper-level management approvals for trade memberships and subscriptions, by restricting specific benefits to senior management, and by routing and sharing publications across business areas.
- ◆ The bank's business meal costs had been growing at a compound annual rate of almost 50 percent—more that 40 percent faster than the growth of staff. By establishing a corporate policy statement with clear instructions and limitations on employee meals, the bank was able to reduce such costs by 30 percent.
- ◆ Travel and entertainment expenditures were similarly reduced by 25 percent through higher-level approvals and consolidation of travel agencies.
- ◆ Simply requiring employees to reimburse the bank for personal long-distance telephone calls and restricting phone service access reduced total long-distance charges by 10 percent. Furthermore, renegotiating and lengthening the contract with its long-distance carrier saved more than $125,000 annually.
- ◆ Centralizing the purchase of personal computers and software, consolidating these purchases through a single vendor, and eliminating the purchase of individual maintenance contracts reduced the annual growth of the bank's computer equipment and software expenditures from 17 percent to 3 percent per annum.
- ◆ Establishing a policy that centralized armored car and messenger deliveries and reduced courier frequencies and routes cut expenses by 15 percent.
- ◆ Centralizing materials management and consolidating purchasing and warehouse functions reduced the bank's overall office supply, postage, and printing costs by 18 percent.

The cross-bank component of the redesign effort is not reengineering. Many of the changes are simply commonsense adjustments to existing behavior that come from a comprehensive review of the bank. The financial impact of this effort is, however, a significant by-product of the reengineering effort.

Top-Down Approaches for Repricing

Linking price to value provides the foundation for generating repricing options around broad-based themes. It provides a basic framework for comprehensively and creatively reappraising the bank's fee pricing at the microtransactional level. Under the value umbrella, however, several dominant repricing themes emerge.

Streamlining Product and Service Offerings

To enhance the revenues of each product line, group leaders and working team members streamline the bank's product and service offerings. They reduce the number of overlapping products exhibiting only slight differences from one another, and eliminate products and services with low customer usage, leading to substantially improved economics. One bank, for example, discovered that its branches still supplied more than 100 distinct deposit account products—"grandfathered" from earlier acquisitions—to specific categories of customers. Eliminating these accounts increased revenues by $3 million annually.

Revenues can also be enhanced by simplifying product delivery and standardizing various transactions to attain higher levels of cost efficiency. Customer relationship analysis can show the extraordinary amount of embedded cost that exists in tailoring products and services to the specific needs of individual customer groups. Standardizing transactions and simplifying product delivery by limiting the degree of effort employees make in satisfying the needs of individual customers can materially reduce these costs. Several examples will help to illustrate how this has been done.

Standardizing products and implementing corporate pricing for savings accounts in one bank added more than $333,000 in additional revenues. Extending the policy to its money market funds added another $1.4 million. And implementing a standard policy at all branches to charge customers a $5 fee for interim statements increased revenues by another $28,000. In total, these repricing options produced over $1.75 million in enhanced revenue for the bank.

The personal trust department of another bank standardized its affiliate fees for all personal trust services. The change involved a 10 percent increase in fees charged overall and produced more than $300,000 in new revenue. A third bank's commercial liability products area standardized business checkbook charges and checking fees corporatewide to generate $388,000 in additional revenue.

Charging for Tailored Service

In some situations, a more tailored approach to service is necessary (for example, where the bank's unique brand of service and superior ability to meet the needs of customers contribute greatly to its market position or enable it to retain its most valuable customers). Increasing the price of transactions to compensate for the additional costs incurred may be appropriate. Referring to the value pricing charts created earlier and carefully reexamining the relative position of the bank with respect to its competitors help significantly in this process. The following are some ideas that have been implemented by banks to recapture the cost of tailored service:

- One bank's commercial liability management instituted a per-customer fee for credit investigations and audit confirmations that generated $1.8 million in additional revenues. It instituted a $5 fee for business checking account telephone inquiries that added an additional $250,000. It also implemented a monthly charge for obtaining an account analysis statement to generate another $130,000. The changes produced almost $2.2 million in annual revenues for the bank.

- The consumer liability products area of the same bank generated more than $50,000 in additional revenue by instituting charges for branch hold and interim statements, telephone transfers for checking and savings, and ATM customer service research.

- A personal trust department instituted a $5 charge for producing account statements other than annual statements, which yielded over $100,000 in new revenues. Another $100,000 was produced when an hourly rate of $125 was implemented for personal services such as financial and estate planning performed by trust officers.

- The wholesale asset area of another bank instituted a $1,000 charge for all asset-based lending field exams. The policy generated over $190,000.

By the same token, where the level of tailored service offered is retained only to compete with other institutions in the marketplace which offer a similar type of service (such as a purchase protection plan offered as a credit card enhancement), the option of raising price in order to dissuade customer use should also be seriously considered. One bank found that it could almost completely eliminate the costs associated with its purchase protection plan by raising the annual fee charged to customers subscribing to the plan. The policy change had no impact on the overall number of credit cardholders.

Tiering Prices

Group leaders use the information gathered through customer relationship analysis to review the potential for repricing products and services to reflect the size of customers' balances or volumes of transactions—that is, price tiering. Those customers having the highest balances and the lowest trans-action volumes often contribute the least to the bank's overall cost. Charging customers with lower balances and higher transaction volumes more for specific products and services can, therefore, enhance the revenue of product lines without risking the loss of the bank's most valuable customers. To achieve its full potential, this form of differential pricing should be applied to the individual transaction components of each product to help ensure that the price ultimately charged reflects the actual costs of low-balance/high-volume users. The following are examples of tiered pricing ideas that have been instituted by banks:

- The consumer liability products area of one bank introduced a low balance fee on all current accounts with balances less than $200 (including direct deposit customers) to generate $1.3 million in additional revenue. Increasing the quarterly fee on savings accounts with balances less than $100 from $2.50 to $5 provided another $220,000. A $5 low-balance maintenance fee on personal money market savings accounts provided an additional $315,000. Increasing withdrawal fees on low balance accounts from 20 to 25 cents per item yielded another $330,000. In total, tiered pricing added $2.2 million in revenues.

- Another bank's commercial liability management tiered the earnings credit on business checking accounts so that the first $5,000 or less in balances earned the standard earnings credit rate less 100 basis points. This produced over $510,000 in additional revenue. A third bank implemented the same policy, but only for accounts with collected balances of less than $25,000, to yield $120,000 in new revenue.

FIGURE 8.4

Value Pricing Consumer Liability Products: Money
Market Accounts

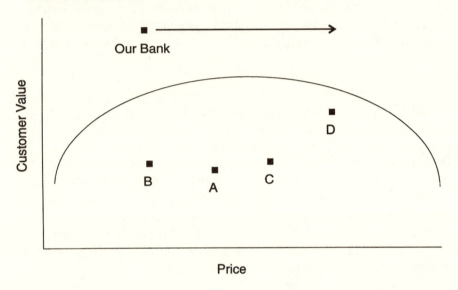

To achieve the maximum revenue impact from this repricing theme,
group leaders and working team members apply the concept of tiered
pricing to each of the bank's major business areas at the product component level.

Identifying New Pricing Opportunities

A rich source for new pricing opportunities can be found by reexamining
the results of the surplus value potential charts completed earlier. The
objective is to charge additional fees for each of the bank's products and
services that are of relative high value to the bank's customers. To illustrate,
the perceived customer value of one bank's money market accounts (see
Figure 8.4) exceeded that of its key competitors, whereas the price charged
to customers trailed them. Group leaders used this information as the basis
for increasing the price charged for the product and generated $400,000 in
revenues.

The following examples illustrate additional instances where perceived customer value has served to justify charging a higher price:

- One bank's retail credit department was able to institute a $150 application charge for home equity lines of credit based on the superior value of its product. The measure generated more than $600,000 in additional revenues. Charging a $10 annual renewal fee for such lines added $220,000.
- The perceived value of another bank's safe deposit box product allowed it to increase pricing by 50 percent, generating more than $400,000 in additional revenues.
- Charging a $2 fee to all nonbank customers for check cashing privileges yielded a bank more than $1 million in revenues.

An additional source of new pricing opportunities comes from unbundling prices for each of the bank's tailored services—rather than charging a fee for a specific product or service, charging a separate fee for each of its subcomponents. Pricing products in this way has the effect of appropriately charging those customers who habitually make unnecessary service demands more than customers with low transaction levels. For example, rather than charging one fee for cash management, a fee might be charged for each type of transaction. Heavy users of telephone-inquiry resolution, for example, can be made to pay for this high-cost service. The following examples will further illustrate how unbundling has been accomplished:

- Rather than imposing a monthly umbrella charge on corporate trust clients, one U.S. bank charged separate fees for subproducts that reflected the underlying cost of providing each. More specifically, it charged for investment management, custody, administration, and 401K record keeping.
- On the personal trust side, the bank charged separate fees for each of the subproducts of its estates and court trusts product. In addition to a base fee it charged an administrative fee, an investment fee, a transaction fee, real-estate advisory fees, and estate administration fees.
- Another bank's commercial liability products area charged separate fees to its demand deposit account clients for maintenance, checks paid, and deposited items.
- On the consumer liability products side, the same company instituted annual, setup, closing, and access fees on its safe deposit box product. It had previously charged only for initial setup of the service.

Last, in exploring new pricing opportunities, group leaders help design new products that can be delivered by leveraging the bank's existing resources. Doing so offers each business area a fresh source of revenue and helps to enhance the overall profitability of specific product lines. Because there will be very little, if any, basis for pricing these products initially, group leaders approach pricing conservatively until an adequate amount of information can be gathered to evaluate the level of each product's success.

For example, at negligible incremental costs, one bank began marketing a pro forma revocable trust product by leveraging its existing trust business that yielded $150,000 of revenue; it unbundled estate services to attorneys for $100,000 in fresh revenue. It also began offering a money market fund to outside mutual funds that did not have a product of their own; upon obtaining just one new account, the bank increased its revenues by $400,000.

Limiting Fee Waivers

The last key issue when exploring repricing options is how to address the inordinate amount of the bank's revenues lost annually to fee waivers. Limiting the number of occasions that customers are relieved of their obligation to pay fees allows the bank to eliminate the chronic abuse of escape clauses for specific groups of customers. One bank, for example, discovered that these waivers amounted to over $4 million in lost revenues out of a total potential income of about $80 million. Hardwiring fees and only selectively granting waivers reduced that number to under $1 million. In other situations, the recoverable lost revenue from waivers has been as high as $6 million but never less than $1.5 million.

Each of the broad-based themes provides the pricing team with a basic framework for addressing the cost and value issues uncovered by the analyses discussed in Chapter 7. Based on the specific characteristics of each business area, group leaders and working team members develop a portfolio of as many as 500 to 750 repricing ideas centered around these themes.

In an effort to further refine the idea portfolios and be certain that the bank's most valuable customers are not overburdened by the combined effect of the pricing changes proposed, group leaders then reexamine the data compiled earlier on market dynamics and runoff and perform two additional analyses: analysis of probable runoff; and burden analysis.

Analysis of Probable Runoff

Employing the results of the historical runoff review completed earlier, group leaders quantify the likely runoff and net revenue impact of each proposed repricing. By examining the expected reduction in number of accounts, account balances, transaction volumes, and the resulting net revenue impact at various price levels (for example, a 10 percent increase, a 20 percent increase, a 30 percent increase, and so on), the pricing team can more easily assess how reasonable the changes they propose are and revise them accordingly. Because the degree of runoff may vary with the size of the price increase, this analysis quantifies price sensitivity and helps set the overall boundaries and risk profiles for the proposed price changes. Some examples will help to illustrate how this has been done:

* Table 8.4 illustrates how one bank arrived at a 60 percent increase in its ATM fees. The net revenue impact generated by this increase—$150,000—was the greatest among the various price increases considered despite the fact that the probable runoff was slightly higher than for a 20 percent or 30 percent increase.

* Another bank determined that an increase in monthly checking fees from $7 to $10, or almost 43 percent, could generate an additional $60,000 in revenues with virtually no account runoff. On its interest-bearing checking accounts it also discovered that a 50 percent increase in its minimum balance fee—from $9.50 to $14.50—could generate another $60,000 with less than 1 percent runoff.

* A third institution determined that, by increasing its per-deposit item charges on business checking accounts from 15 cents to 17 cents, or by about 13 percent, it could generate additional revenues of over $30,000 without any runoff.

Burden Analysis of Proposed Pricing Changes

Burden analyzis establishes the degree to which individual customer segments are affected by the cumulative impact of proposed pricing changes. Group leaders calculate the change in fee burden and overall contribution of each customer segment across all product lines and compare the relative burden borne by each segment. This prevents the bank's most valuable customers from bearing a disproportionate share of the burden as a result

TABLE 8.4

Runoff Analysis of Proposed Pricing Changes—Consumer Liability Products: ATM Fees

Price Change (%)	Revenue Base ($ Millions)	Expected Volume (Millions)	Probable Runoff (Millions)	Runoff Impact ($ Revenue)	Related Balances/Assets ($ Impact)	Net Revenue ($ Impact)
20	1.05	3.45	0.05	12,500	50,000	112,500
30	1.14	3.30	0.20	50,000	100,000	115,000
60	1.40	3.19	0.30	75,000	300,000	150,000
100	1.75	3.04	0.46	115,000	650,000	110,000
At today's price	0.875					

FIGURE 8.5

Burden Analysis

Percentage of Price Increase Borne by Customer Segment

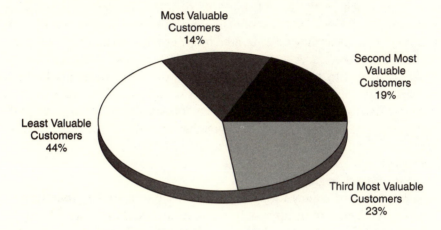

Most Valuable
Customers
14%

Second Most
Valuable
Customers
19%

Least Valuable
Customers
44%

Third Most Valuable
Customers
23%

of proposed pricing changes. In situations where the most valuable customer segments are affected disproportionately, group leaders and working
team members revise the pricing idea portfolio accordingly.

Figure 8.5 illustrates the effect of one bank department's portfolio on
each of its customer segments. As shown, the bank was ultimately able to
develop an idea portfolio in which the burden of price changes was progressively greater for the bank's least valuable customers.

Top-down direction of idea generation built around broad reengineering themes for both cost and pricing is, therefore, a critical part of reengineering. This is supplemented by bottom-up option generation that focuses
more on redesign of tasks down the line that are affected by the overall
process redesign themes.

Bottom-Up Approach

Potential bottom-up sources of ideas include: the database of objectives and
tasks and their associated costs, jump-start ideas, brainstorming sessions,
the systems liaison, and input and ideas from other groups.

Objectives and Tasks Database

The database of objectives and tasks should be scrutinized carefully, as it is often a valuable source of ideas and certainly identifies those areas on which the most resources are spent. In banks with parallel organizational structures (such as those with multiple affiliates or data centers), it is interesting to compare the cost of achieving objectives among the duplicative functions. Ideas may be generated if one group's costs are significantly higher than another's. Alternatively, group leaders may question why the objective needs to be accomplished in two different locations. Perhaps combining the operations of the two groups would yield substantial savings with low risk to the organization. There are obviously many other comparisons and analyses which can be performed on the set of objectives and tasks that yield equally rich reengineering options.

Jump-Start Ideas

Smaller, microefficiency ideas can also be used to help the group leaders jump-start the bottom-up approach. Aston Associates has compiled lengthy summaries of ideas that have been considered for each area of the bank, but these can also be brainstormed by senior management. The jump-start ideas are not directives, but merely suggestions to help the group leaders examine every aspect of their organization and processes.

Brainstorming

Brainstorming sessions are an excellent means of encouraging idea generation among all the members of a group. These sessions can be used most productively when the group leader designs a process statement that may focus on one of the group's objectives or on a central theme. Participants in the brainstorming session are invited on the basis of their involvement in the selected process. Employees from all levels of the organization should be encouraged to participate in these sessions in order to provide the maximum number of different perspectives on an objective or theme.

One of the principal rules of brainstorming is that no idea is to be discounted. What appears to be a bad idea may simply not have been adequately expressed. Even seemingly unworkable ideas may serve as catalysts for generating other ideas. In addition, more ideas are likely to be generated in a positive environment than in a negative one. There are many ways to kill an idea (as illustrated in Table 8.5); it is much more difficult to nurture an idea until it becomes workable. The important thing to remember is that no idea is too small to be considered. This is the time to consider all ideas for productive change in the bank.

TABLE 8.5

Thirty Ways to Kill an Idea

1. We've tried this already.
2. That's too risky to try.
3. These savings do not affect my budget.
4. Who is going to pay for that?
5. The auditors/regulators won't like that idea.
6. If it's that good, why hasn't somebody tried it before?
7. We only do this because XXX requires it.
8. That's a short-term solution. We must look into the future.
9. That's a long-term solution. We live now.
10. XXX will never buy it.
11. The way we do this is the most effective—otherwise we would be doing it differently.
12. That's not my problem; it's somebody else's problem.
13. This is a radical departure from industry practice.
14. You would never get the customer to agree.
15. Why don't you apply this in other departments? They really need help.
16. But what about the effects on other divisions?
17. That's contrary to company policy.
18. It may be OK for others, but our situation is different.
19. I've been waiting for people to do that for a long time.
20. I don't have the staff to do this analysis.
21. In theory you may be right, but in practice . . .
22. We need XXX's approval; I'm sure he's against it.
23. Oh yes, you can improve anything with numbers.
24. Users of my services would never accept that.
25. We've always run a lean operation.
26. Why should we be interested in combining our activities with Department XXX?
27. This whole exercise is unnecessary.
28. Why should I share this resource?
29. It will take years to implement this.
30. We've already got enough to meet the 40% target.

The Systems Liaison

The systems liaison is a valuable resource for generating automation ideas and for ensuring the efficiency of new or existing systems across groups. The systems liaison can also help the group leader estimate the cost of implementing a new system or automating a task in an existing system.

Other Groups

Last, the group leader examines ideas generated by other groups to judge if any of them have applicability to his or her own group. This is an ideal way to ensure that best practices are shared and applied across the organization.

After the group leaders have compiled their portfolios of reengineering options, they must carefully estimate the impact of those ideas. In particular, they must identify:

- The amount of savings or revenues generated by an option.
- The one-time costs if any of implementing it.
- Any continuing costs it may entail.
- Any negative revenue impact of cost-reduction ideas.

Group leaders also assess any intangible benefits of the idea, any potential adverse consequences, and issues to be taken into consideration when implementing the idea. They also provide their own assessment of the risk of each idea. Through this process overall bank portfolios of over 5,000 individual ideas for change (large and small) have been developed, all capable of implementation within a year of the reengineering design.

REFINING OPTIONS

When initially creating the idea database, the group leaders should record each idea. After this process, however, the group leaders must refine the portfolio of options to weed out those ideas that are not appropriate. Because the focus of the effort is to redesign the organization, ideas such as "reduce the chairman's salary by 50 percent" violate the principle of the process and should be discarded. Some ideas will not qualify for the target. The pricing groups cannot count cost-saving ideas toward their goal, and cost groups cannot include revenue-generating ideas in their portfolios. Ideas that create savings in areas not part of a group's baseline budget are not eligible; they are passed along to another group leader but cannot be used to meet the first group's target. Ideas that cannot be completed within a four- to six-quarter implementation period are also not considered for purposes of the target. (This is to avoid large projects that create big up-front costs with only a promise of savings sometime in the distant future.)

Last, the group leader must review and refine the costing of each idea to ensure accuracy and avoid double counting. Some ideas will generate an overlap in savings or revenues. Each of these ideas must be evaluated incrementally because the same dollar can be saved or earned only once.

Evaluation of the Options

To take into account the complex interdependencies inherent within a bank's cost and pricing structures, evaluation of the ideas by all affected parties across the bank is a necessity. Idea evaluators should always include the group leader, the responsible working team members, the group leader's functional or line-of-business manager, and the management committee. Other evaluators may include the suppliers to the group, the users of the group's products and services, and requestors of information generated by the group.

Each evaluator is asked to comment on the idea; to suggest ways to improve it; and to judge whether the option involves low, medium, or high risk. To help the group leaders "upgrade" ideas, evaluators are asked to state specifically the type of risk involved. Risk types may include credit risk, market or customer risk, and implementation risk. If an evaluator views an idea as being medium- or high-risk, then he or she must suggest a way to improve it, in order to lower its risk.

Input from the management committee is especially important. Members of the management committee meet individually with each pair of working team members to discuss the larger ideas within each group's idea portfolio. The purpose of these sessions is to familiarize the management committee with all the more significant ideas and allow its members to provide input at an early stage of the evaluation process, thereby building a base of support for controversial ideas. The management committee meets with the working team three times before the decision-making stage, in order to upgrade ideas continually and produce a portfolio of many low-risk, high-benefit ideas.

The evaluation process must be carefully monitored to avoid "analysis paralysis." The process should seek ways to improve the ideas, not to delay their development.

The goal of idea evaluation is to lower risk and generate options. It is not necessary to gain consensus for each idea. Evaluators may legitimately have different opinions. The role of the group leader is to research potential risks, weigh them against benefits, and present as many options as possible.

Upgrading Ideas

Because ideas with medium- or high-risk ratings are less likely to be approved for implementation by the management committee, a formal stage in the program is provided for idea upgrading. The idea evaluation process should identify all the potential objections to a reengineering option. The upgrading process develops modifications and alternatives to counter these objections and reduce risk.

One method of lowering the risk rating of a particular option is to break the idea down into lower- and higher-risk components. In this way the lower-risk idea may still be implemented, even though the higher-risk idea is rejected, and the portfolio will thus maximize the overall cost and revenue impact of implemented ideas.

SETTING THE NEW BANK'S COURSE

During an intensive period the management committee meets to review all the reengineering ideas and to decide which to implement in partnership with the sponsoring managers. During this period the management committee devotes 100 percent of its time to the decision-making process until every idea generated has been reviewed and decided upon. The group leaders present the reengineering ideas in each of their portfolios and discuss the merits of the ideas at individual sessions. There are really no surprise ideas, because the options have been reviewed repeatedly by evaluators throughout the bank, particularly by the management committee. There will still be some controversy around specific ideas, however, and the management committee will solicit input in order to resolve a debate and make a decision. The management committee uses this forum to challenge risks, to raise issues, to find ways to increase the impact of the program, and to ensure the consistency of the overall corporate design.

The management committee will ultimately make a decision on every idea, approving or rejecting each for implementation.

IN CONCLUSION

The reengineering design phase of the program takes about four to six months for a midsized regional bank, two to three months for a smaller bank and six to nine months for a larger institution. It is by definition an intense experience but also an exciting and challenging time for the bank. Staff develop a sense that they are really creating a new bank in a "no-holds-barred" environment where every process and tradition can be radically changed. The organizational energy released is awesome to observe.

CHAPTER 9

Creating the New Bank

INTRODUCTION

Creating the new bank from the ideas approved by the management committeee is the centerpiece of reengineering. If implementation of these ideas has not been management's focus from the outset, then the program has failed. The keys to successful implementation are detailed planning, linkages to normal management processes (such as the budget), and rigorous tracking of results.

PLANNING THE FUTURE

To plan effectively for the future, a concerted effort must be made to implement all facets of the approved reengineering program (Table 9.1). This includes four basic steps:

- Determining the "capturability" of personnel and nonpersonnel savings.
- Reflecting the savings in the budget.
- Developing action plans for large or complex ideas.
- Reviewing the remaining organizational structure to uncover further delayering opportunities.

TABLE 9.1

The Six-Step Approach to Reengineering

Step	Major Components	Chapter
Preparing for change	Psychological preparation Cost preparation Repricing preparation	7
Understanding current processes	Understanding processes and costs	7
Understanding current pricing	Contrubition analysis Product workflow analysis Unit cost derivation Customer relationship analysis Value analysis	7
Generating reengineering options	Top-down approaches for process cost design Top-down approaches for repricing Bottom-up approach	8
Refining options	Evaluation of the options Upgrading ideas	8
Charting the new bank's course	**Planning the future Tracking achievement Avoiding execution pitfalls Re-commitment of the new bank**	**9**

Determination of "Capturability" of Savings

Capturability involves translating the cumulative savings of staff time generated by the approved ideas into the elimination of full-time positions. During this part of the planning process, the group leaders develop creative approaches to organizational design to achieve 100 percent capturability by using part-time employees, combining positions (within and across groups), reorganizing process and workflow responsibilities, and redesigning job specifications.

Consolidation into the Budget

Once the capturability of savings is determined, the group leaders and their managers, in conjunction with the implementation coordinators, convert the results of the reengineering program into the bank's budget system. The first step is to unravel responsibility centers from the group aggregations.

The savings or additions of FTEs, personnel expense, and nonpersonnel expense are then allocated to the appropriate responsibility centers and revised budgets are developed.

To realize the impact of the pricing ideas, the pricing team develops a matrix that allocates the value of each pricing idea to appropriate groups and their respective responsibility centers.

Design of Action Plans

Group leaders are also responsible for developing individual action plans for those ideas that generate significant savings or revenues or that require more complex implementation. These plans identify the milestones for smoothly and successfully implementing the ideas, their deadlines, and the staff members responsible for accomplishing each step.

One role of the action plans is to identify evidence of bottlenecks or inconsistencies among the ideas for implementation. It is the responsibility of the implementation coordinators to consolidate issues across groups and prioritize the implementation of ideas so that the required resources can be made available.

Realization of Delayering Opportunities

The group leaders are responsible for creating new organization charts for their groups, to outline how their areas will look during and after implementation. Senior managers are responsible for evaluating the consolidated organizational charts for their departments. To create the most efficient organization possible, they carefully consider the reasonableness of reporting relationships and the resulting organizational structure as these factors relate to process workflow. Spans of control are increased and unnecessary layers of management removed. Last, the refined organizational charts are reviewed by the management committeee.

In the same way that senior middle managers rationalize reporting relationships among the groups of their departments, the management committeee evaluates the overall organizational structure of the bank. As a result of the redesign ideas being implemented, existing reporting relationships may no longer make sense. This presents an opportunity to create a truly new organizational structure, allowing every aspect of management to be reviewed.

TRACKING ACHIEVEMENT

Implementation of the approved ideas is undertaken by the group leaders and their managers during the four to six quarters immediately following the conclusion of the reengineering design phase. During this period, the role of the implementation coordinators is to oversee the responsible parties to ensure the timely and effective implementation of all reengineering programs.

On a biweekly basis initially, and each month thereafter, the management committeee holds meetings at which the implementation coordinators update the management committeee with regard to the progress achieved by each group, as well as the status of each action plan. Because the action plans identify the parties responsible for achieving each milestone, this process ensures strict accountability. These review sessions also serve to resolve any issues that cause delay resulting from conflicting priorities among groups.

AVOIDING EXECUTION PITFALLS

To make a reengineering program of this magnitude work, there are several issues to which senior management must pay close attention.

Revisiting Costing

Group leaders and division executives will most likely find myriad reasons why approved ideas should be reopened for discussion, or the savings or revenue projections of those ideas changed. With a multitude of individual action plans, the management committeee will never be able to assess whether a requested change is legitimate or a smokescreen. It must, therefore, take the position that modifications will be entertained only with rigorous justification. In every one of the reengineering programs that I have undertaken, the common experience has been that 90 percent of the ideas were, in fact, undercosted or understated due to conservatism during the idea development and refinement phases.

Because the bank has assigned its best managers to the reengineering effort, the management committeee should consider the total savings estimate of each group to be a binding contract. Any shortfall of savings or revenues in one idea, therefore, must be made up by the impact of others.

Resisting Reinvestment Pressures

Any reinvestment proposal of $50,000 or more should be presented to the management committeee in a formal, consistent fashion as part of the biweekly updates. Requests not showing a positive variance to the year's budget should be rejected unless an overwhelming business case demonstrating their need can be made to the management committeee. Tracking the revenues and expenses of approved reinvestment decisions then becomes part of the implementation coordinators' mandate.

Undermanaging Hiring

In support of the first two points, rigorous controls on hiring are critical. Through at least the first quarter of implementation all new recruitments should be approved by the management committeee. Thereafter, such approval for exempt positions should continue.

In addition, at the biweekly update, the implementation coordinators should present a summary of the reengineering program's progress which compares the target FTE status to the actual numbers by personnel category. Careful attention should be paid to any variances and the responsible parties held accountable.

Lacking Repricing Discipline

Perhaps the hardest ideas to track are those relating to waivers of fees. The implementation coordinators need to identify all the waiver/noncollection ideas, indicate how they will be tracked, and specify how "offenders" will be identified.

Lacking Ownership of Cross-Bank Ideas

There is a danger that many of the cross-bank ideas may lack clear ownership (such as the expenditure discipline for travel and entertainment). One remedy is for the implementation coordinators to take personal responsibility for the cross-bank idea portfolio. Some of the larger ideas also need to be supported by a clear statement to responsible executives that their performance evaluation depends on achieving the agreed-upon savings and that a significant portion of their incentive compensation will be linked to full realization of those ideas.

Selecting the Wrong Implementation Coordinators

The implementation coordinators play a significant role in ensuring the successful implementation of the reengineering program. Selecting the appropriate individuals for these positions is, therefore, critical. In particular, the implementation coordinators should be perceived internally as leaders who will handle the politics of monitoring realization of ideas across the bank. They should be creative, determined, and tactful, yet not unduly political. Particularly, they should be able to handle sensitive, internal meetings without creating a political uproar. The implementation coordinators will also need the support of a dedicated analyst, whose responsibilities are: to work with the human resources team to track the actual realization of the headcount on a weekly basis, to monitor realization of nonpersonnel cost reductions, to track implementation of the repricing initiatives, and to police the milestones for implementing big ideas.

RECOMMITMENT TO THE NEW BANK

Once the organization has been reengineered and streamlined for the future, serious attention must be paid to boosting employee morale and enthusiasm. Up to this point the environment will have been one of uncertainty, followed by the stress surrounding tough personnel decision making. When this phase is complete, however, the success of the effort and ultimately of the bank depends upon reigniting employee commitment to beating the competition.

Recommitment sessions chaired by members of the management committee are a useful means of introducing the scope of the redesign ideas to all managers even if they are not directly affected. This is an opportunity for the management committee to describe the interdependencies involved in the implementation process and to enlist the support of these "thought leaders."

The new organization must function as a team, with senior managers playing the role of coaches. If a senior manager is not committed to achieving the benefits of the new organization, he or she cannot effectively recruit others and, therefore, may not have a role with the new bank.

Potentially, the most unifying aspect of the new organization is that it will have been created by all of the bank's employees. Although not every employee will agree with every decision made, the value of each person's contribution should be recognized. Simple morale builders such as buttons or posters can be effective tools in communicating the bank's new cultural dynamic to employees.

This positive attitude has its greatest benefit in what is communicated to the customer either through customer interactions with employees or through employee contact with the media. Customers should continually receive the message that the mission of the new organization is intently focused on having more streamlined processes, less bureaucracy, and overall improved customer service (rather than having a "we don't do that here anymore" mind-set). Ensuring that staff deliver this positive message can, and should, be actively managed and constantly reinforced.

IN CONCLUSION

Reengineering is not about lengthy reports by outsiders sitting on shelves gathering dust. Rather, it is about focusing the latent appetite for change that exists in every bank in order to create a new institution. The proof is in the effectiveness of implementation.

Case Studies

To demonstrate the power of reengineering, three case studies will be helpful: CoreStates Financial Corporation of Philadelphia, Pennsylvania; Lincoln First of Rochester, New York; and Star Banc Corporation of Cincinnati, Ohio. These three institutions have been chosen because they all were superior performers before they embarked on a fundamental redesign of their processes and economics. It took courage and vision for Terry Larsen, William Balderston III, and Oliver Waddell to lead their organizations through the intense reengineering experience necessary to win against competitors in the 1990s and beyond. Moreover, for each bank, a published article exists that offers a view, other than my own, of reengineering: for CoreStates and Star, *American Banker* reviews; and for Lincoln, a piece from *The Banker's Magazine* by William Balderston III.

As I have said, the challenge of reengineering an already top-performing bank is far greater than that of reengineering a troubled institution, and also often produces more lasting results. These three case studies are a testament to this phenomenon.

CHAPTER 10

CoreStates Financial Corporation (Philadelphia, Pennsylvania)

"CORESTATES PAINSTAKINGLY PUTS ITS IDEAS TO WORK" [1]

A row of 18 thick binders rests on a long credenza in the president's office at CoreStates Financial Corp. The neatly arranged volumes contain what is essentially a blueprint for a massive restructuring project begun last August. Over seven months, the Philadelphia-based bank collected and evaluated more than 6,000 ideas for cutting costs and improving operations.

The $28.5 billion–asset company approved 3,500 of those ideas, which are expected to produce significant reductions in expenses ($180 million), employees (2,800), and branches (10 percent) when they are implemented over the next 12 to 18 months. The process was "difficult" and "tough"—but also necessary—said Charles L. Coltman III, president and chief operating officer. "This is an industry that's headed for significant, ongoing consolidation," he said. "We're facing new competitors, different competitors, new demands from customers. And we need to be prepared for those changes."

But while the tough decisions were made by the end of March, CoreStates now faces perhaps the more formidable job of putting thousands of ideas into practice with a minimum of damage to the corporate culture. "CoreStates was, and is, a fascinating organization that is committed to a

---

1   By Jeffrey Zack. Reprinted with permission from *American Banker,* July 10, 1995.

fundamental cultural change," said Paul Allen, chairman of Aston Associates, the Greenwich, Connecticut-based consulting firm that assisted in the reengineering. The bank, he said, was well along in "the process of moving from a centralized, paternalistic, blame-driven culture toward one where they are aiming to empower employees close to the customers to make decisions."

Major bank restructurings such as CoreStates' have been getting headlines for years. But the Philadelphia bank is among the growing number of institutions that are undertaking these programs from a position of financial health. The bank's first quarter return on average assets was 1.63 percent, excluding one-time charges. Return on equity during the period was 19.64 percent. The reported return on assets (ROA), including the $110 million pretax charge, was 0.79 percent, compared with –0.44 percent a year earlier, a figure that included a merger-related charge.

Analysts have praised reengineering efforts that seek to improve efficiency, but some voice skepticism that banks are focusing on cutting costs at the expense of building revenue over the long term. Critics say these reengineerings have the more immediate goals of calming investors and avoiding takeover bids. CoreStates's program, known as BEST (Building Exceptional Service Together), however, has received higher marks than some other bankwide restructurings. Nancy A. Bush, an analyst with Brown Brothers Harriman in New York, said: "It's the best-engineered program of this kind that we've seen" because it is not geared only toward cutting costs. "It's not a slash-and- burn program, which some of the other programs have ended up being," said Paine Webber's Thomas McCandless. "I think they went about it the right way and came up with an intelligent and conservative plan."

But the admiration is qualified. Ms. Bush noted that the bank's timetable for reaching the goals was considerably longer than the timetables of other programs. "Eighteen months is a lifetime in the banking industry these days," she said. And Mr. McCandless said, "We just have to see how the execution flies." Mr. Coltman insists, though, "We will accomplish the numbers that we have put out to the analysts."

Indeed, the executives were unusually frank in sharing details with analysts about CoreStates' plan, and a desire not to disappoint Wall Street may help explain why the bank established a longer-than-usual implementation phase. Mr. Coltman also conceded that the major technology investments and changes needed to meet its goal lengthened the timetable. "There is back-end loading of the results in our project because it will take some time for the systems group to make their changes internally," he said. "That's not something where you can snap your fingers and get done." Of the 3,500 ideas CoreStates is pursuing, some 460 involve technology. Together, they are expected to result in $44 million in savings annually, about 25 percent of the total.

"There are some areas that we really need to make some major investments in," said Mr. Coltman. "There is a lot of moving from a traditional bank mainframe structure in our systems delivery into client/server technology." CoreStates has budgeted $30 million for new technology, including an imaging system for the proof-of-deposit function in its check-processing operations. Such investments in technology are necessary to remain competitive, he said, particularly for Transys, the bank's third-party processing subsidiary. Mr. Coltman also said the bank would spend to develop alternative delivery channels for the retail bank to compete against the likes of Pennsylvania rival Meridian Bancorp, which had gained a reputation as a leader in that arena.

To achieve these goals, CoreStates' reengineering has followed a by-now-familiar path. The bank brought in consultants—Aston. A top level executive—Mr. Coltman—acted as the "sponsor." Other company managers—some 26—worked full-time on the project. Some 71 group leaders, along with other bank employees, were charged with contributing ideas that simplify processes and speed up the flow of work. The five most senior executives reviewed each idea and set up a plan to implement the suggestions that were approved. "We went into this saying: 'We need to look at every single thing we do, see how we do it, and see whether it adds value to our customers,'" said Mr. Coltman. "And if it doesn't, stop doing it."

The savings are expected to come from steps both small and large. Some, said Mr. Coltman, were easy. Branches, for example, continue to take pictures of checks before they are sent off to be processed. CoreStates' policy was to change the film at the end of each week. Now the film is changed as needed. "That idea alone is going to save $12,000 a year," said Mr. Coltman. Quarterly reports mailed to shareholders had been very detailed. Now, the bank sends a shorter version which reduced the paper, production, and postage costs by 83 percent. The cumulative savings of such ideas, according to Mr. Coltman, ran into the millions of dollars.

One major area of savings was in slashing the number of reports generated for internal use. "We had a very complicated, detailed, profit-center system that allocated expenses and revenues down to groups as small as five or six people," said Mr. Coltman. CoreStates plans to cut the number of those "profit centers" from 1,900 to 125. Among the benefits: savings of $500,000 a year in paper costs. (The bank is also investing in new management information systems to generate more meaningful data.) The biggest saving, presumably, will come from reducing the workforce by 19 percent, or 2,800 employees. Fewer employees, along with fewer branch offices, also means CoreStates can substantially cut costs—by some $18 million, or 10 percent of the total—through the consolidation of office space.

Taken together, these measures can mean big savings. But managers concede they do not come without risks. "The impact on revenue, the impact on the internal culture, the impact on the customer were things we worried about going in," said Mr. Coltman. "And they are things we continue to worry about." Whenever a company laid off people, he said, morale inevitably suffered. But he noted that the workforce reductions were largely achieved through attrition and voluntary departures. Fewer than one-third of the layoffs—843—involved pink slips.

Mr. Coltman also acknowledged that morale at the bank was still recovering. "Things are slowly moving back on the upswing," he said, "but I would also say that we still have a long way to go before we can look back and say the process is ended."The bank also tried to be fair when it made layoff decisions. "It would be based on [employees'] performance in the past, it would be based upon their leadership around the core values of our company," said Mr. Coltman.

"Any fundamental redesign change program is going to be threatening and intense for employees," said Aston's Mr. Allen. "The question is, how do you structure and tailor the redesign process in any bank to minimize those things? CoreStates was dedicated to telling their employees everything as soon as they knew it."

Another risk was that streamlining operations could impair customer service quality. So each idea was assigned a rating to gauge its impact on the customer and on the bank's culture. "There were a number of ideas where the customer risk just seemed too excessive, and we pulled back," said Mr. Coltman. For example, process changes in the commercial lending business suggested that loan officers could be responsible for many more accounts than they had been under the old system. "We decided not to go that far," said Mr. Coltman. "In some cases, we only went half as far as the pure analysis suggested."

As the various measures are implemented, CoreStates' team of "implementation coordinators" is also looking for unintended consequences. In those situations, the bank will forgo the change. "That's something that we've learned from watching other reengineerings," said Mr. Coltman. "There is a process in place to make sure that there is not too negative an impact." Management also hopes that an organizational change resulting from the reengineering will help the bank keep an eye on customer needs.

Previously, management had been organized around lines of business. Now, the delivery of all products is divided into four geographic regions. The presidents of each of the four regions, along with the senior managers for corporate and retail delivery, report to Rosemary B. Greco, president and chief executive of the lead bank. "Their job is to look at the entire delivery process of their segment across all four markets and to design product for specific market segments within that," said Mr. Coltman. That reorganization followed last August's trimming of the senior policy committee from 13 executives to 5. The current members are Terrence A. Larsen, chairman and chief executive; Mr. Coltman; Ms. Greco; Charles P. Connolly Jr., senior executive vice president; and Robert N. Gilmore, chief technology officer.

Although Mr. Coltman said the bank's reengineering was at times grueling—the five senior executives met for nine consecutive 12-hour days to consider the 6,000 ideas—he had high praise for the process. "One of the key decisions you make around reengineering is: 'Do you want the reengineering accomplished over a long time or over a short time?'" said Mr. Coltman. "And while I would say that probably every one of our working team members would say the seven months we took was 'too short,' everyone would also say, they wouldn't want it to have been any longer."

CHAPTER 11

Chase Lincoln First Bank (Rochester, New York)

THE POSITIVE SIDE OF RESTRUCTURING[1]

"**R**estructuring"—a buzzword for banking in the 1990s—instantly brings several questions to mind: what is it like to experience such basic change, and how are banks avoiding organizational bedlam? What makes it work and what lasting results can banks expect? During 1990 and 1991, Chase Manhattan discovered the answers to these questions. It undertook an aggressive restructuring with the aim of reducing staff by 5,000 and noninterest expense by $300 million—goals that the bank was able to achieve.

Chase approached the challenge of restructuring in myriad different ways, fitting the approach taken to the different strategic, business, and social conditions in its various global locations and lines of business. In each case, the bank set a hurdle to ensure consistency in cost and staffing reduction with the long-term strategic importance to shareholders of the individual business or location. In some instances, a realistic, hard-nosed evaluation of profit potential revealed that divestment was a necessity; in others, the bank's leadership position or potential called for a net investment, rather than any downsizing.

---

1   By William Balderston III. Reprinted with permission from *The Bankers Magazine*, March/April 1992.

Regional banking in the United States provides an interesting combination of these strategies for illustrative purposes. The business is a core strategic priority for Chase Manhattan, but the bank knew that only an optimal cost and revenue structure could provide the springboard to make it a leading player in the wake of industry consolidation. Thus, as part of the overall corporation's objective, senior management at Chase Lincoln First Bank, Chase Manhattan's upstate New York bank, prepared during 1990 for a fundamental change in the bank's economics and in the way all its employees did their jobs. The institution's goal was to achieve the changes through "rightsizing," not through an arbitrary downsizing.

The Chase Lincoln First example shows how one approach to change enabled Chase Manhattan to achieve its restructuring mandate in a positive, energizing fashion rather than as a morale-destroying, knee-jerk response to market pressures. A detailed review of the Chase Lincoln First experience may be of interest to others considering the path of reengineering.

Ways to Improve Productivity

As senior management at Chase Lincoln considered the rightsizing objective, in January 1990, it saw that the bank had an opportunity to improve productivity dramatically. To do so, it set the following guidelines:

- Senior management would not impose across-the-board cost cutting.
- The tasks each employee performed would undergo comprehensive evaluation to determine whether they added value for the customer and to the bottom line.
- Although achieving major expense reductions and revenue improvements would be the absolute goal, jeopardizing customer service or revenue or taking undue risks would not be tolerated.
- Because employees would be asked to identify redundancies and inefficiencies in their own jobs, they would participate in the decision making to give them an ownership stake in the changes the bank would face.

To achieve the objectives, the bank clearly had to change the way it did business. The whole organization had to undergo fundamental change, including each and every management process and operational system.

The financial results of Chase's efforts have been dramatic. By the end of 1991, the $6 billion asset institution had added more than $33 million to pretax income. Other things remaining constant, this income would increase return on assets (ROA) by 35 basis points and return on equity (ROE) by more than 500 basis points. Using the bank's fourth-quarter 1991 running rate as a base, this performance will amount to more than $41 million in pretax income in 1992 and, with other factors constant, will add 44 basis points to its ROA and approximately 600 basis points to its ROE. This improved performance is being accomplished without selling assets, exiting businesses or closing branches. In addition, these financial achievements are being realized without a sacrifice in service quality.

The bank could not have produced these results without a unique approach to accomplishing this radical rightsizing. Restructuring is about creating energy and commitment in an organization, managing the fundamental change involved in questioning everything about the way things were done in the past, and involving everyone in the process.

The bank's overall conclusion was that, although a disciplined, comprehensive technical approach is critical to focus the energy released during restructuring, three other factors were key to the bank's success:

- The bank created a "partnership" to accomplish the change and fortunately picked the right partner (Paul Allen of New York and his team).
- Senior management was absolutely committed to change and stood behind it.
- The change process was managed as a line effort.

Choosing the Right Partner

Chase Lincoln's goal was to distinguish itself from its competitors and become the cost-effective leader in providing banking services to its market. Accomplishing this goal would entail more than the usual budget cuts or productivity enhancements adopted by most banks; rather, it required a companywide commitment to radical operational change. Management decided early on that such an undertaking could succeed only with the help of an outside resource—a partner, in effect—who could guide the bank's staff to challenge conventional wisdom, set ambitious goals, and embrace change.

To fill this important role, Chase Lincoln chose Paul Allen, a New York City–based expert in bank restructuring. Paul Allen and his team brought to the effort their experience in multiple bank restructurings, their analytical skills, and their ability to remain objective while sharing management's commitment. The team worked on-site with all levels of the bank's staff throughout the six-month effort. They helped the staff to explore the implications of radical change, provoked debate among senior management, maintained a focus on key goals and unified all levels of the bank behind a strong commitment to change. Chase Lincoln is convinced that the energy and drive unleashed through its partnership with Paul Allen was one of the crucial factors in the success of its efforts.

Beginning the Change

The entire restructuring process was called "A+Plus." At the start of 1990 the bank was performing well but was only in the middle of its peer group. Senior executives graded the bank as B minus but were determined to make it a superior performer.

To do so, senior managers had to understand and be committed to fundamental change. The bank executives created a team of its best people, selecting indispensable managers to lead the effort. They communicated frankly and comprehensively across the bank to challenge the entire staff to participate in the process of change.

Before top management notified anyone of its A+Plus program, the bank's top 10 managers spent a month with Paul Allen and his associates in an intensive meeting, during which they challenged the need for the effort, became comfortable with the proposed approach, and ensured that they would be able to manage a controlled disruption of the business while A+Plus was progressing. Paul Allen's expertise helped establish rational expectations for A+Plus, introducing some organizational stability despite the uncertainty about where the project would lead the bank.

Perhaps most critical was the process of prioritizing other strategic initiatives and accepting that some of them would have to be placed on the back burner while A+Plus was made the highest priority for the bank. Treating restructuring as an incremental task for employees to juggle along with all the usual demands on their time would have undermined the restructuring. Delaying pet projects also becomes an acid test of the sponsoring executives' commitment to the restructuring program.

Involving the Best People

Managing, motivating, and monitoring A+Plus rested with a seven-person steering committee consisting of Chase Lincoln's senior executives. The steering committee was ultimately responsible for making decisions on recommendations. One senior executive whose track record and temperament ideally suited the project's goals was appointed to lead A+Plus. A working team of 20 men and women representing the major business lines as well as support and staff functions was selected from the bank's best and brightest employees. They played the key liaison role with the 50 work group leaders who drove the project down the chain of command to gather input from almost every employee.

The working group did the detail-oriented work in their areas of expertise and the teams were then assigned line items of expense that cut across the bank and were not controllable by any one group. The teams examined costs associated with such expense categories as equipment, occupancy, travel and entertainment, and data processing and systems development. On the revenue side, the bank named pricing teams for each major business line and turned them loose to develop ideas on potential sources of incremental transaction fee income.

Telling It to the Staff

Selling A+Plus to employees was not easy. Over the years, the bank had gone through the usual cost-reduction programs. The existing business environment was difficult, however, and other banks were taking a pounding in the press. Combining the usual amount of organizational skepticism with unfavorable industry publicity increased the risk of creating a volatile situation. Asking people to identify wasteful activities in their own jobs called for a delicate and comprehensive communications plan and a carefully managed human resources initiative.

A+Plus was launched at concurrent meetings in each of the bank's seven geographic regions. Senior regional executives handled the presentation in their areas, working from a common script and video tape. The basic theme emphasized the reasons the bank needed to make the change and also emphasized everyone's role in creating a new bank that would be a more effective provider of financial services and a more profitable competitor.

The bank regularly sent each employee a special A+Plus communication piece that included answers to questions. Each steering committee member and all the working team regularly surveyed the staff for concerns, which were then candidly discussed in the A+Plus update. Updates were published every three weeks and distributed bankwide.

The bank also elected to bring this story to the news media to neutralize the negatives that often develop when reporters are given inaccurate information.

In addition to open and frank involvement of the staff, the A+Plus program involved a comprehensive and sensitive human resources plan.

Employees whose jobs were eliminated were placed in a pool and these people were given priority consideration for positions opened by normal turnover. This arrangement facilitated the phased staff reductions that were part of the A+Plus implementation.

Although the trauma of potential staff layoffs can never be wholly removed, the open discussions, the involvement of the employees, and a sensitive approach to their concerns and their future enabled the employees to view the A+Plus program in as positive a light as possible.

A Line Effort

The magnitude of A+Plus's success at Chase Lincoln First was largely a result of the fact that the program was, in both fact and perception, driven and directed by employees as a line management effort. The project exhaustively reviewed each and every task employees performed daily with a special emphasis on low-value activities. No area was immune to review. From chairman to custodian, in every nook and cranny, expenses were scrutinized. Similarly, employees analyzed fees in terms of the individual transaction value to the customers of each unbundled service that the bank provides. They carried out rigorous evaluations of the specific price sensitivity of each transaction to reestablish the link between the fee charged and the value perceived by the buyer of the service.

To encourage a full and honest accounting, the A+Plus program established a stretch target—one that demanded a great deal of thought and effort from the employees. Managers mandated employees to produce idea portfolios affecting their entire budget (both personnel and nonpersonnel expenses and revenues). The target challenged employees to think deeply and be creative while the bottom-up process gave them the safe harbor of knowing they had some control over their destiny. Qualifying ideas passed from the working groups to the group leaders, who validated each proposal based on:

- Implementation timing (a five-quarter maximum).
- Implementation expense (correctly quantified).
- Savings expressed on an annualized pretax basis.
- Agreement from units affected by implementation.

Expense savings from the ideas generated were balanced with their impact on revenues. Although in all cases improving the value of work done or charging for the value provided was paramount, compromising service quality was forbidden.

To accommodate control and service quality issues, all areas affected by each proposed change were asked to rate the risks involved. After being risk-rated and validated, ideas flowed through the pipeline to the final test: passing muster with the steering committee. The results were staggering. Employees generated more than 7,000 ideas which exceeded every expectation. By any measure, Chase Lincoln employees had successfully turned the bank on its head. They created a revolution of ideas aimed at revising the old way of doing things, and they helped to establish the new way.

For seven days, the steering committee considered recommendations prepared and presented by the working groups. The committee looked at the ideas one by one and then accepted, rejected, or modified them, or sent them back for refinement. The working group leaders were active and passionate advocates for the ideas they presented. The whole senior management team was focused on every area of the bank—for both the micro-bank and cross-bank issues. For seven solid days, and often late into the night, these people held lively (and sometimes acrimonious) debates and thought-provoking discussions.

Some Implemented Ideas

Approximately one-third of the ideas made the grade for implementation. Suggestions for improving productivity included eliminating management layers to get closer to customers, rebalancing account loads, outsourcing back-office functions, and streamlining the annual planning process—along with hundreds of others. The text below presents some of the recommendations for broad changes that were accepted and implemented.

Pricing to Customer-Perceived Value

Changes included increasing stop-payment fees to match competitive charges, actually collecting branch research and copying fees that were normally not billed or collected, instituting a transfer-out fee for individual retirement accounts (IRAs), charging a low-balance maintenance fee to recover costs, raising fees on life insurance trusts and for tax preparation, and 150 other transaction fee changes.

Pruning Demand Deposit Products

Analysis of this line of business revealed products with similar features for which there was a low level of customer interest. As a result, the bank eliminated coupon book and savings bond products and other demand deposit items. This action resulted in sizable savings in the bank's information systems department because the number of computer programs that required maintenance decreased significantly.

Rationalizing Lending Processes and Procedures

Efforts to streamline these activities resulted in quicker decision making on loan applications, more sharply defined accountability for lending, redesign of some credit forms and automated production of them, reconfigured lending teams (composed of senior and junior relationship managers, account administrators, and customer service representatives), and adjustment of account loads to meet market needs more effectively.

Eliminating or Reducing Dual Controls

Each of these $5,000–$10,000 ideas changed the way the bank did such things as loading ATMs, maintaining safe deposit boxes (including changing the locks), controlling safe deposit keys, and processing night deposit bags.

Streamlining Administrative/Operating Activities

The A+Plus program led the bank to take greater advantage of outsourcing. For example, payroll services and PC support functions were outsourced. Also, the program led to more purchases of off-the-shelf software. Before, the bank had developed software that was already available for such tasks as managing the float and measuring computer cycle times in mainframes. Other cost savings were derived from the elimination of reports for which there was not much demand and of manual logs for official checks, as well as automation of the sales tracking input process and account maintenance (for example, changes of addresses and names).

Centralizing Customer Service

The bank created a service unit for customers in which they could call a toll-free telephone number to reach trained customer service representatives who had access to computerized customer records. This change resulted in faster customer service because visits to a branch to inquire about balances or check clearing were no longer needed. More important, it freed up bank personnel to spend more time on other tasks, particularly for intensive product selling.

When the bank began implementing the new policies, separations began feeding into the well-oiled human resources program that had been established at the outset. Although staff anxiety was inevitable, the openness of the process, the forthright communication to those affected, and the investment in internal and external placement removed some of the uncertainty and fostered a sense of fairness across the bank. Morale remained surprisingly positive as employees gained a new sense of focus directed toward what was most important in serving the bank's customers.

Looking Ahead, Glancing Back

In 1990 Chase Lincoln First's senior management team committed the bank to a rigorous self-examination to assess its ability to meet successfully the challenges in an increasingly complex and competitive environment. Because the bank was reasonably healthy and profitable, the approach could be resolute but not a fire drill. This is not to suggest that A+Plus did not promote organizational anxiety. Plenty of participants (even in the senior management ranks) had plenty of misgivings going into A+Plus and made a few missteps along the way. However, A+Plus delivered—or more accurately, the team of management, staff, and Paul Allen delivered the hoped-for results.

CHAPTER 12

Star Banc Corporation (Cincinnati, Ohio)

STAR GETS AN OVERHAUL TO BOOST PERFORMANCE[1]

Despite its name, Star Banc has spent most of its 120-year history building a reputation as a buttoned-down institution that avoided the spotlight whenever possible. But recent events, particularly an unsolicited acquisition offer in 1992 from its Cincinnati rival, Fifth Third Bancorp, have Wall Street and other industry observers paying closer attention to the $7.4 billion asset company.

Star's mission is to make those suddenly interested investors forget about Fifth Third's hefty $42-a-share offer by accelerating its efforts to increase revenue and capture greater back-office efficiencies.

"One of the things I have found annoying is that Fifth Third is getting credit for all the economies we're putting in," said Oliver W. Waddell, Star's chairman. "But the Fifth Third offer added more importance to what we were doing and probably stepped up our time schedule a little bit," he acknowledged. "Any organization in a competitive marketplace has to take steps to operate more efficiently. Star has been doing that," said Stephen Mead Jr., a research analyst at the money management firm, Anchor Capital Advisors, in Boston.

---

1   By Brian Hellauer. Reprinted with permission from *American Banker,* June 21, 1993

But he added that events also "heightened management's awareness that it has to actively sell the stock" to be better able to fend off unfriendly advances and maintain the confidence of its board of directors.

Once it decided that good performance was no longer good enough, the bank stepped up its housecleaning in 1992. Star executives say this restructuring, dubbed "Project Excel," will contribute $30 million to the company's annual pretax earnings after it is fully implemented in 1993.

Investors appear to agree, because Star's stock was trading in the mid-$30s earlier this month, rebounding from $29 after the Fifth Third rebuff in 1992.

"You're seeing companies doing this all over the place," said Mr. Waddell. "But most of them are doing it as they're getting ready to fail, because they've got major problems. We did it, and we had no major problems. We're taking what is a good bank and making it an exceptional bank."

Star defines exceptional as consistent returns of more than 1.25 percent on assets and 15 percent on equity. That represents a significant jump over Star's traditional performance, typically in the neighborhood of 1 percent ROA and 12 to 13 percent ROE. Waddell (age 62) and Star have also begun preparing for a change of command. In May 1993 Waddell stepped down as CEO, a position he had held for a decade. The bank then reached outside its management ranks and named Jerry A. Grundhofer as president and chief executive officer of the holding company. Grundhofer is a former top-level executive at BankAmerica, Security Pacific, and Wells Fargo.

"I didn't come to Star Banc to babysit it," said Mr. Grundhofer, adding that he was just beginning to familiarize himself with the bank's day-to-day operations.

"This is a great franchise with a first-rate management team. There are lots of opportunities to use this as a springboard to continuing improvement. Our mandate is to increase shareholder value. I know how to do that," he said. Still, implementing the many changes that Star made in its effort to become a superior performer was neither quick nor easy, noted Waddell.

Star had been trimming fat from its systems and operations as far back as 1987. At the time the company, known as First National Bank of Cincinnati, consisted of the lead bank and 22 acquired affiliate banks in two states. This loosely knit aggregation produced steady if unspectacular results.

Star spent several years closing redundant item processing centers in the affiliates, standardizing products, and taking other steps to streamline operations. The company also added substantial acquisitions in Cleveland and in a third state, Kentucky.

The Excel project, management thought, would take Star's efforts to another level. Star's management committee hired an outside firm, Aston Associates of Greenwich, Connecticut, which specializes in bank restructurings.

"What I liked about it was that this program was administered by Paul Allen [Aston's chairman], and maybe four other people on his staff, which meant the majority of the work had to be done by us," said Waddell. "It wasn't like having a consultant who does everything for you and then goes away."

Nor was Aston afraid to shake things up. During Allen's initial presentation to the management committee, he asked that Star's top 17 managers be assigned to the project exclusively for the three months. "I said, 'We can't do that. This whole organization is going to come to a screeching halt.' Then he started packing up," Waddell remembered. "I said, 'What are you doing?' He said, 'I'm leaving. It's obvious you're not sincere about what you want to do here.' That kind of shook us up a bit."

The management committee was further rattled when it tried to identify the Star employees who would temporarily replace the 17 managers. "We didn't make it halfway through the list. Paul said the only way we were going to know what sort of backup we had was to let him have the people. That I found very intriguing," Waddell said.

The demands made of the managers involved in the project were no less stringent. Members of the team examined an area of the bank removed from their normal field of expertise.

"All of us had a lot of confidence to do what we had been trained to do," said Thomas J. Lakin, an executive vice president who was one of the senior people involved with the project. "We were suddenly disconnected from that and put in a room where all 17 of us worked together for three months, with a lot of pressure, trying to get things done. It was an unbelievable experience." As an example, Lakin, who had spent his entire 27-year career in Star's trust department, was assigned to review some retail banking and administrative functions.

"The logic behind that is, we don't want people coming in with a bias or vested political interest in seeing business conducted as usual," said Paul Allen. "These people start asking questions and find that products, processes, and systems are derived from something that made sense 10 years ago." The Excel team worked with department heads in what Lakin called "a reengineering exercise." Each department had to develop a list of suggestions to reduce expenses by 40 percent and to increase revenue by the same percentage.

"The 40 percent was an unreal number. We knew that going in," said Lakin. "But it forces you to think of ways to come up with the 40 percent without blowing the place up."

The exercise generated a stack of volumes containing 2,500 suggestions and filling several feet of shelf space in Lakin's office. These ideas were rated according to risk and presented to the management committee over a two-week period at the end of 1992. Most of the suggestions and the subsequent changes were related to staffing and organizational issues.

"The efficiencies, the economies are really in the structure—trying to get decision making closer to the customer and taking the administrative burden out of the affiliate banks," said Joseph Campanella, an executive vice-president and management committee member, who supervised the Excel project. Campanella also noted that most of the changes within the bank over the previous year related to a number of broad themes.

One Bank, One State

Under the new arrangement, the network of affiliate banks is being dissolved in favor of a single bank charter in each of the three states where Star operates.

Line-of-Business Management

Rather than maintaining separate profit-and-loss statements for each affiliate, Star reorganized its accounting to match its eight lines of business, which are managed from its headquarters.

Centralized Administrative Functions

In addition to accounting, other administrative functions were brought into Star's Cincinnati headquarters.

Selective Price Hikes

The revenue-generation portion of the Excel project involves raising fees on various bank products and services based on what Allen called the "perceived value" of the products to the customers. Although increased fees are often met with complaints from annoyed customers and negative publicity, Allen says the runoff caused by such increases is less than 1 percent.

Implementing these changes was not a painless process. The Excel program will eventually reduce the job count at the bank by 450. "The greatest areas we hit were out in the field. The affiliates had a rougher time of it," said Lakin.

Employees whose jobs were being eliminated were informed as soon as the decision was made even though some of those jobs would not be eliminated for up to a year after the announcement. That decision was based on fairness to the employee, said Lakin. If the bank was going to cut the workforce, it was willing to risk low morale or early departures.

Displaced workers are also being given first shot at positions that open up in the bank through normal attrition. Nevertheless, Mr. Lakin said the layoff was tough. "It still is," he said. "It will take a while, if ever, for the organization to get over that."

A number of affiliate presidents also resigned shortly after the reorganization, reportedly upset over their loss of autonomy. Star Bancers argue that the "delayering" of management will improve customer service. "We've cut out layers, and we've gotten it down," said Waddell. He said that lending decisions would typically involve one or two officers at the most. "Hopefully, we can give much faster and much better service."

"There are three things that came out of this: the expertise of our people, the ability to make acquisitions work faster, and the skill level that's been built for continuous improvement," said Lakin, who was named to the management committee. He will continue to co-manage the Excel project through the end of the year.

"The easy way, which some banks take, would have been to say, 'Gentlemen, we're going to cut 20 percent right across the board,'" said Waddell. "There you're throwing the baby out with the bath water."

So far, the bank is performing as expected. In the first quarter Star reached its self-determined milestones, posting a 1.35 percent ROA and 16.48 percent ROE. Analysts are guardedly optimistic. "I was skeptical of Excel when the numbers first appeared. It seemed like an overly ambitious view," said Joseph Duwan, an analyst with Keefe, Bruyette & Woods, New York. "But they had a great first quarter on the cost side. It will be interesting to see how things develop on the revenue side."

The spate of recent moves seems to indicate Star's desire to remain independent, even in a market that is filled with healthy, aggressive competitors. "You all keep trying to sell us," said Waddell, referring to rumor mongering by analysts and the media. "I hope you aren't successful, but you may be." Whether Star goes it alone or not, its experience demonstrates that in banking, as in boxing, staying in fighting shape can be a rigorous business.

■ ■ ■

To give a feeling for the specifics of the Star Banc reengineering, I thought it might be helpful to outline some of the redesign components of just one area: Systems and Operations. To avoid lengthy text descriptions, this will be achieved using the exhibits that follow. They capture graphically the scope of change achieved over the four-month reengineering design phase. (See Figures 12.1 to 12.6, and Tables 12.1 and 12.2.)

FIGURE 12.1

Reengineering Systems and Operations—Process Overview

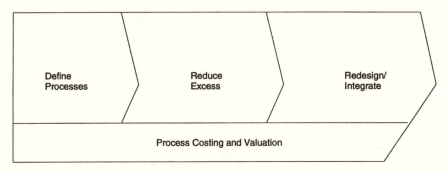

* 20% annual cost reduction

* Improved customer service
  - Availability of information/services
  - Accuracy of information
  - Speed of response

* MIS projects and support closely linked to
  business and internal customer requirements

FIGURE 12.2

Reengineering Systems and Operations—Key Success Factors

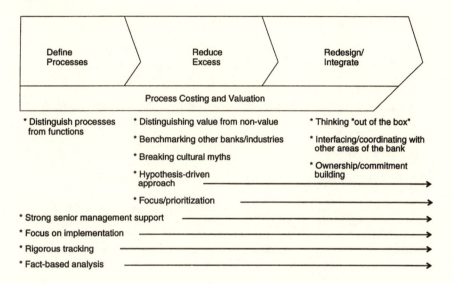

FIGURE 12.3

Reengineering Systems and Operations—Understanding Current Processes

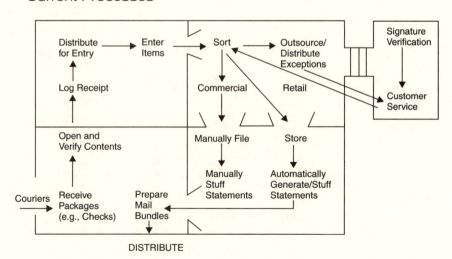

TABLE 12.1

Reengineering Systems and Operations—Reduce Excess

Challenge/Hypothesis	Findings	Result
Mailing cost per piece was higher than for other companies doing local bulk distribution.	Alternative vendors could distribute bulk mail for significantly less.	Savings of $180K/team, and faster, more reliable service.
Fed fees paid were well in excess of best practice institutions.	The package sort model used was out of date.	Savings of $54K per annum.
The volume of reports printed was greater than the resources available to use them.	About one-half of the reports generated were never used.	Paper costs alone could be reduced $33K per annum.
The cost of the signature verification process was greater than its value to the bank.	The signature verification group had not identified a single fraudulent item nor contributed to any legal defense in the prior five years.	Staffing was reduced by 67%, focused on high-value items, and trained accordingly.

TABLE 12.2

Reengineering Systems and Operations—Redesign/Integrate

Challenge	Opportunities Identified	Annual Savings ($000s)
Optimize an existing activity.	Minimize the number of sorts and sorter "clicks" by minimizing sorter batch size.	25
Resequence the activities in an existing process.	Redesign the item storage area and procedures.	25
	Bulk-file manually filed items.	30
Challenge the underlying assumptions of the process.	Combine DDA, savings, and MFP statements.	120
	Offer check information to both retail and commercial customers.	350

FIGURE 12.4

Reengineering Systems and Operations—Define Process Historic Organization and Activities

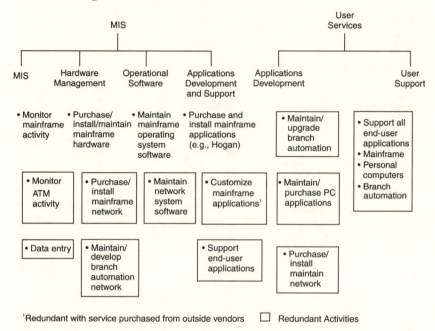

¹Redundant with service purchased from outside vendors   ☐   Redundant Activities

FIGURE 12.5

Reengineering Systems and Operations—Process Overview

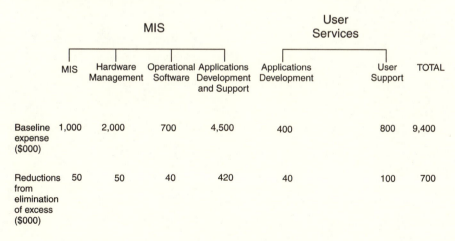

	MIS	Hardware Management	Operational Software	Applications Development and Support	Applications Development	User Support	TOTAL
Baseline expense ($000)	1,000	2,000	700	4,500	400	800	9,400
Reductions from elimination of excess ($000)	50	50	40	420	40	100	700

FIGURE 12.6

Reengineering Systems and Operations—Redesign/Integrate

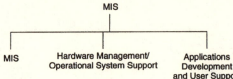

MIS

MIS	Hardware Management/ Operational System Support	Applications Development and User Support

* Monitoring functions redesigned to reduce cost and improve efficiency

* All technical support merged under one umbrella

* Strategy for integrating personal computer and main-frame defined

* Available technology fully leveraged

* Process-aligned development/ support teams created

* Application modification request process refined to focus resources on key business needs

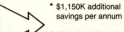

* $1,150K additional savings per annum

* More flexibility and beter reesponsiveness to business requirements

The Future of the Banking Industry

I am astounded by the pessimism of many banking pundits—not to mention bankers themselves—in discussing the future of the industry. Take, for example, the number of times such terms as "obsolete," "unnecessary," "disintermediated," and "out of date" have been used in the media; this alone would lead one to believe the global banking system is a dinosaur on the verge of extinction.

In truth, bankers have many competitive advantages on which to build: a unique distribution network coverage of branches, ATMs, and loyal, highly- trained salespeople in what has essentially become a local retailing business; sophisticated payments, transaction processing, and securities and foreign exchange trading technology and skills; superior credit underwriting capabilities; and, most important, the exceptional loyalty and inertia of consumers, small business owners and the like.

Since the mid-1970s, industry critics have been predicting the demise of banking. And, in some ways, the industry has been its own worst enemy, whether because of developing country loans; highly leveraged transactions; real estate credits; or other expensive product fads such as discount brokerage and, potentially, mutual fund acquisitions. Yet, based on its competitive strengths, the industry has always bounced back. Nevertheless, bankers are under siege. They cannot afford to be complacent about their record earnings in 1992–1996 (excluding Japanese and French banks), nor about their underlying basic business advantages.

One market in which banks are probably becoming obsolete is basic commercial lending. Access to capital market alternatives is stretching across all maturities for all but the riskiest borrowers. But, even here, bankers can use their superior underwriting skills to embrace the new technology of securitization of loans to establish a defensible role.

Nonbank competitors are becoming fierce invaders of what have traditionally been the most profitable core banking markets. This is true for consumer assets where credit cards, auto loans, and mortgages are being supplied by firms in the United States such as Dean Witter, GMAC, and Lomas Mortgage, USA—with cost structures designed specifically for product niches. It is also true for consumer liabilities where disintermediation is accelerating to mutual fund suppliers such as Fidelity, and to discount brokers such as Charles Schwab which have national brand franchises. And even control of the payments system is challenged by firms such as Electronic Payments Systems and electronic data interchange firms such as GEISCO.

Pricing pressures (at least for explicit, balance-related rates) are mounting, as shown by the collapse of the credit card interest rate umbrella, the flight from certificates of deposit, and the squeeze on domestic and international cash management and payments charges.

The supernormal earnings of 1992–1996 are not sustainable in the medium term, as a revenue crunch caused by the above factors will squeeze traditional earnings.

All these trends point to one key message which, for me, has not changed since this book was first published: the industry has to get its house in order by adjusting its economics to meet the challenge of product specialists, and to compete successfully against them.

This is not a matter of incrementalism. It is not a case of using minor fixes to improve efficiency marginally so as to do the same old things at a slightly lower cost. Banks must radically redesign their basic processes and business approaches to reflect the realities of competition in the 1990s. They must reengineer the bank in order to survive and thrive. And the examples of successful reengineering, such as that at CoreStates, First Security, and Star Banc, prove that this is not wishful thinking.

CEOs with the vision and courage to face the economic realities of their industry are empowering their staff to redesign the bank from scratch. They are using the resulting improvements to the value of their stock to fund acquisition and using the discipline instilled throughout the bank as a result of the reengineering process to realize the consolidation benefits so often lost in the past. They are tackling the new entrant intruders head-on, and they are winning.

True reengineering, nonetheless, is not easy. It involves challenging each precept of traditional banking and remolding an institution's culture. Yet, if structured and managed as outlined in this book, it can be an exciting and reinvigorating experience that melds the institution—be it large or small—more tightly together, while returning its focus to that of customer sales and service.

Banks can be winners in the new millenium. They can meet and overcome the challenges they face. To do so, however, they must confront the reengineering imperative immediately. For it is a critical part of the formula for a bank's survival and success.

A Reengineering Lexicon

Action Plans   A detailed plan of implementation for each approved reengineering program. An action plan identifies the steps required to implement the idea, a timetable for completing each step, and the person or persons responsible for accomplishing the steps.

Baseline Budget   On the cost side, the controllable and ongoing (personnel and nonpersonnel) noninterest expenses of the entire bank. On the pricing side, the ordinary and ongoing revenues generated from each of the bank's main businesses and product lines.

Bundled Pricing   A method of charging a customer based upon the overall number and level of services used rather than on the usage of each individual service, product, or transaction.

Capturability   The process of translating the estimated number of staff members saved by an approved program into full-time position reductions.

Common Costs   Expenses that are shared by different customer segments for multiple products across dispersed locations.

Competitor-Based Pricing   A method of setting prices to charge customers that matches the prices charged by competitors. Competitor-based pricing does not take into account the customers' price elasticity of demand.

Contribution Analysis   An explicit cost/benefit analysis to determine the amount of profit generated by the bank's products and services detailed at the subproduct level.

Cost Interdependency   The degree of overlap between and among a bank's management and infrastructure cost levers. Cost interdependencies cause a change in one area of the bank to have a ripple effect throughout the organization.

Cost Levers   The determinants of common costs (processes, functions, plant, systems, and overhead) that serve multiple customers, products, and geographies.

Cost-Plus Pricing   A method of setting prices to charge customers based upon the cost of production plus a profit margin. Cost-plus pricing does not take into account the customers' price elasticity of demand.

Cross-Bank Analysis   A horizontal examination of line-item costs in the bank's budget which affect the organization across all groups. It complements the vertical examination of processes by groups.

Customer Relationship Analysis   A detailed analysis of the transaction volumes, costs and revenues associated with each customer segment by subproduct. The purpose of a customer relationship analysis is to detect any imbalance between the cost of service levels provided to specific customer groups and the revenues obtained from them.

Delayering   The process of removing unnecessary layers of management between senior management and the customer by increasing the number of reporting relationships for middle managers, and analyzing and streamlining the resulting organizational structure.

Group   The basic analytical unit for the reengineering process formed from responsibility centers on the basis of similar processes, functions, or markets.

Group Leader   A manager of one of the responsibility centers composing the group. The group leader is responsible for gathering, analyzing, inputting, improving upon, and presenting the data and recommendations from reengineering to the management committee.

Idea Database   A collection of ideas gathered from top-down sources (such as the management committee) and bottom-up sources (such as the objectives and tasks database, jump start ideas, brainstorming sessions, the systems liaison, and other groups).

Idea Evaluation   The review of each idea by all affected parties across the bank in an effort to identify the level of risk involved in implementing the idea.

Idea Refinement   The process of improving the idea database by cutting out inappropriate ideas and ideas that do not qualify for the stretch target and challenging remaining ideas on their costing, implementation requirements, and adverse consequences.

Idea Upgrading   The process of improving each idea, based upon the user evaluations, to generate alternative ideas with lower risk and/or increased savings or revenues.

Implementation Coordinators   Two or three people appointed by the management committee to oversee the preparation for, and implementation of, the reengineering process.

Infrastructure Levers   Levers of common costs that cut across business and organization structures. The five infrastructure levers are processes, functions, physical plants, systems, and "pure" overhead (such as matrix management costs and senior management "perks" and incentive compensation).

Jump-Start Ideas   A set of microefficiency suggestions used to give the group leaders a "jump start" in generating a database of ideas.

Management Committee   The senior executives of the bank who are responsible for directing and guiding the reengineering process.

Management Levers   Axes of strategic and organizational management that drive bank costs. The management levers are: customer segments, products, and geographies.

Market Analysis   A thorough analysis of the price elasticity of demand in a given market area.

Microefficiency Ideas   Cost-saving or revenue-generating options that focus on doing the same things in a better way or at less cost. In contrast to redesign ideas, microefficiency ideas tend to focus on tasks, rather than processes.

Objectives   The reasons for a group's existence. Objectives answer the question "why" a process exists.

Perceived Customer Value   The importance a customer places upon a product and/or its attributes that underlie the relative price elasticity of demand.

Process   "A collection of activities that takes one or more kinds of input and creates an output that is of value to the customer."[1]

Product Attributes   The characteristics of a product or service, defined as the fulfilment of specific needs. Examples of product attributes include speed, accuracy, security, and confidentiality.

Product Workflow Analysis   A diagram of each step in the production of a product developed to identify the various (open and hidden) cost components associated with that given product.

Redesign Ideas   Cost-saving or revenue-generating options that focus on doing "better things." In contrast to microefficiency ideas, redesign ideas challenge why a process is performed, focusing on the process rather than the tasks that constitute that process.

Reengineering   "The fundamental rethinking and radical redesign of business processes to achieve dramatic improvements in critical, contemporary measures of performance, such as cost, quality, service and speed."[2]

Relationship Pricing   See *Bundled Pricing.*

Repricing   A systematic approach to examining a bank's products and services in an effort to link prices charged with value provided to the customer within the parameters of the bank's cost of production and competitive environment.

Re-recruitment   Activities designed to seek the recommitment to the new organization of the employees retained after reengineering.

Responsibility Centers   The cost centers, which are the basic building blocks for a bank's budgeting system, that are aggregated to form the baseline budget of each group.

Sacred Cow   A process, product, or service that cannot be examined or altered. (There can be no sacred cows in the reengineering process.)

Skills-Based Assessment   A method for selecting which employees will be retained in post-reengineering positions by evaluating them in terms of those skills required to perform the duties of the new job.

Spaghetti Costs   See *Cost Interdependency.*

Stretch Target   An aggressive goal for achieving a specified percentage of the group's baseline budget as savings. The stretch target is set aggressively to encourage radical thinking, not to mandate a large across-the-board cost reduction.

Surplus Value Potential   The potential for increased revenues that exists when the price of a product or service is less than the perceived customer value.

---

1   Michael Hammer and James Champy, *Reengineering the Corporation,* HarperCollins, Harper Business, 1993

2   Ibid

Systems Liaison   A person appointed by the management committee to provide group leaders and the working team with ideas and information related to the implementation or improvement of automated systems.

Tasks   A set of steps that determine "how" a group accomplishes its objectives.

User Evaluation   The assessment by users of the groups' outputs, or suppliers of information for groups' needs, or requesters of outputs from groups, of the risk associated with implementation of any specific idea.

Value Analysis   A comparison of the value placed upon certain product attributes relative to the price charged for each attribute. The value analysis is used to detect mismatches between price and value (as perceived by the customer).

Value-Based Pricing   A method of setting prices to charge customers based upon the customers' price elasticity of demand.

Working Team   A group of 10 to 20 individuals who are devoted full-time to the reengineering process. The working team is responsible for guiding the group leaders; therefore, each member should possess strong leadership, team-building, and analytical skills.

Working Team Leader   Generally, a member of the management committee, who serves as the point person in anticipating and resolving strategic-level concerns, employee morale issues, and political impediments. The working team leader guides, challenges, and reassures staff so as to move the process to its final goal.